# GEORGE KENNAN

## A Writing Life

## Lee Congdon

Wilmington, Delaware

Congdon, Lee, 1939–

    George Kennan : a writing life / Lee Congdon.– 1st ed.–
Wilmington, Del. : ISI Books, c2008.

        p. ; cm.
        ISBN: 978-1-933859-71-2
        Includes bibliographical references and index.


        1. Kennan, George F. (George Frost), 1904–2005. 2. United
States–Foreign relations–Philosophy. 3. Politics and war–Philosophy.
4. Historians–United States–Biography. 5. Ambassadors–United
States–Biography. I. Title.

E748.K374 C66 2008                      200828616
327.730092                             0811



ISI Books
Intercollegiate Studies Institute
Post Office Box 4431
Wilmington, DE 19807-0431
www.isibooks.org

Manufactured in the United States of America


book design by Union Street Publishing

*to Alex Bandy*

I would rather, really, throw myself into work that was more closely connected with such things as literature and the aesthetic side of life, for which I think perhaps, particularly in the later years of my life, I have greater instinctive understanding.

—George F. Kennan, 1959

# Contents

# Preface

As proponent of the post–World War II policy of containing the Soviet Union, as an architect of the Marshall Plan for European recovery, and as a leading authority on Russia, George F. Kennan occupies a secure place in the history of the Cold War. Every student of that history knows of the "Long Telegram" that, in 1946, he wired to Washington from his embassy station in Moscow. In that telegram, and in his equally famous "X" article, "The Sources of Soviet Conduct," he offered U.S. officials and the educated public an unblinking assessment of Stalin's regime and the way in which it approached dealings with the West. The United States, he argued, should not deceive itself concerning the possibility of friendly relations, but neither should it conclude that a third world war was inevitable. Firm measures would prevent the Soviets from expanding beyond the territory in Eastern Europe that they had occupied as an unavoidable result of the war.

Although for a time he exerted a decisive influence upon the makers of U.S. foreign policy, Kennan soon came up against the tendency of America's leaders to think in military rather than diplomatic terms—and also against an ideological anti-communism suspicious of any contact with Russia. Once the USSR joined the United States as a nuclear power, it was in his view crucially important to keep open channels of communication. Where once he was seen as a rigid anticommunist, Kennan began to be attacked for being soft on communism. No one was more critical of him than John Foster Dulles, President Eisenhower's secretary of state. It was Dulles who wrote an end to Kennan's legendary career in the foreign service; without intending to do so, however, he freed the thoughtful loner for his true calling.

This is a study of George Kennan as a writer, Kennan the author of *Memoirs, 1925–1950*; *Sketches from a Life*; and *Russia and the West Under Lenin and Stalin.* I became interested, in a serious way, in Kennan's life and work in 1981–82, when I was a visiting member of the School of Historical Studies at the Institute for Advanced Study. He was then very much alive, and thanks to a kind invitation from Professor John (J. H.) Elliott, the distinguished historian of Spain, my wife and I dined with the Kennans. Although it was then that I conceived the idea for this book, I still had some unfinished business—the completion of a trilogy on twentieth-century Hungarian intellectuals.

Scholars have written—and will write—much about George Kennan's career in the foreign service, but with the notable exception of John Lukacs they have devoted surprisingly little attention to his life as a writer. As the following pages will make clear, I believe that Kennan wrote because, before anything else, he had genuine literary aspirations. In his writings, both professional and private, he sought beauty of expression as well as self-knowledge or, perhaps better said, self-understanding. Throughout his long years in government, he was painfully aware of the fact that the persona he had assumed for sound professional reasons was not the person he truly was. I have attempted here to portray the real George Kennan.

# Acknowledgments

As George Kennan knew, loneliness is a writer's companion. While working on this book, I have experienced that loneliness with particular intensity, in part as a result of my retirement from university teaching. I am all the more grateful, therefore, to friends with whom I have been able to share my interest in Kennan's life and times. With Kenneth Dawson, who is more like a brother than a friend, I have explored the subject of civilizational decline. From Philip Bigler, one of my finest students and a former National Teacher of the Year who now directs the James Madison Center at James Madison University, I have gained valuable insights into American history. Lawrence Uzzell has always been willing to share with me his vast knowledge of all things Russian. The late David Hallman introduced me, as only he could, to the world of the Southern Agrarians, and I have often turned for counsel to David Bovenizer, who knows everything worth knowing about American conservatism. Theodore Leach has listened to me as a friend.

I am deeply indebted to the Institute for Advanced Study for the hospitality extended to me on two occasions. It was there that I met George Kennan and learned much concerning his life in Princeton. Two of his secretaries, Terri Bramley and Liz Stenard, kindly shared their special knowledge of Kennan as a person. At Princeton University Library, Daniel J. Linke, University Archivist and Curator of Public Policy Papers, gave me the benefit of his expert knowledge and assisted my work in every way possible. I am grateful to him for granting me permission to quote from the George F. Kennan Papers. Special thanks are also due to Jeremy Beer, editor in chief of ISI Books, for his interest in my work, and to my editor for a job well done.

My debt to my wife Carol, my son Mitchell, my daughter Colleen, and my daughter-in-law Jennifer is such that it cannot ever be repaid. Finally, I have dedicated this book to the former AP correspondent in Budapest with whom, over many years, I have enjoyed so many conversations, debates, laughs, and Hungarian apricot brandy. My visits to his and his wife's home overlooking the Danube in Nagymaros, Hungary, always lift my spirits; their friendship is one of my greatest blessings.

*Harrisonburg, Virginia*
*February 2008*

# 1

# The Foreign Service

In 2000, George Kennan published a slim volume titled *An American Family: The Kennans—The First Three Generations.* His purpose in writing the book was to deepen his self-understanding; "such," he observed in his introduction, "is the importance of inheritance and tradition in the determination of personality that without some knowledge of one's antecedents—of the conditions that formed them and of the ways in which they tended to react to those conditions—one will always be lacking in the ability (limited even in the best of circumstances) to understand oneself."[1]

While by no means minimizing the importance of genetic makeup, Kennan was primarily interested in family traditions, those persistent qualities and ways of life which shape character. However singular his life's path may have been, he was convinced that he shared with his forebears certain structures of personality, certain habits of the heart. His genealogical researches—which he had pursued for a great many years— seemed to confirm his intuitions.

The Kennans—originally McKennans—came to the United States from Scotland or Northern Ireland in the eighteenth century. They settled in Massachusetts, but later removed to Vermont and later still to upper New York. Farming was their usual occupation, one that discouraged interest in abstract and theoretical questions and taught practicality. From them, Kennan believed, he inherited his love of rural life and detestation of large cities. Later, the family made its way to the Midwest, to Ohio and then Wisconsin, where Kennan was born on February 16, 1904.

Kennan wrote with particular pride of his grandfather's grandfather, Thomas Kennan (1773–1843), who followed his son John to Ohio in the 1830s. A Presbyterian minister, Thomas Kennan sided with those of his faith who rejected Calvin's doctrine of "total depravity" and who frowned upon the revivalist enthusiasm that Charles G. Finney brought to DeKalb, New York, while he was the local pastor. His, it is clear, was a serious but rationally mediated form of Christianity in which moral rectitude was more important than doctrinal purity or emotional fervor—the kind of Christianity to which George Kennan was always attracted. As we shall see, however, he never forswore a more moderate version of Calvin's view of human nature.

Thomas Kennan shared with other family members what Kennan described as an almost compulsive striving for maximum independence. He recognized this trait in himself and conceded that it limited his ability to form intimate associations with others. No wonder, then, that he and other family members instinctively chose "lonely [professions]—the farm, the law, the pulpit, the pen, and the scholar's dedication."[2] He could have added "the foreign service."

The theme of loneliness, of belonging neither to the century nor the country in which he was born, runs through all of Kennan's writings. He viewed himself as a man apart, an observer of, rather than a participant in, modern life. This distance contributed to a rare clarity of vision, but it also produced a profound feeling of alienation. One can sense this in the personal note with which he began the first volume of his moving and beautifully written memoirs. From childhood on, we learn, he lived "in a world that was peculiarly and intimately my own, scarcely to be shared with others or even made plausible to them."[3]

George Kennan never knew his mother, Florence James Kennan, who died shortly after he was born; from her side of the family, he believed, he inherited his love of the sea. He identified with his tax-lawyer father, Kossuth Kent Kennan, "a man of much loneliness" who managed to liberate himself from the constraints of Puritanism and to open his eyes to beauty.[4] The senior Kennan was named after Lajos Kossuth, the leader of Hungary's failed revolution and war of independence against Austria in 1848–49. Americans came to know the Romantic revolutionary when, in 1851, he accepted an invitation to visit the United States. As a symbol of freedom, he became the first foreigner since General Lafayette to address the House of Representatives—which he did in Shakespearean English!

In the early months of 1852, after having delivered his speech, Kossuth traveled the length and breadth of the country in the hope of raising money for another revolution. Along the way he became the subject of countless newspaper articles and editorials and the object of public adulation. Cities named streets and squares after him and politicians proclaimed him the Washington of the nineteenth century. The country was, for a season, in a state of intoxication.

Despite his name, however, Kossuth Kennan preferred men of the previous—the eighteenth—century; and so did his son. It was as a rather odd duck, then, that, in 1921, Kennan graduated—as class poet—from St. John's Military Academy (Delafield, Wisconsin), an institution that contributed greatly to the formation of his character. It was there that he learned self-discipline and self-respect. "We learned to dress neatly and how to keep a room in order," he said in a speech given at the academy in 1960. "We were *not* allowed to run around looking like hoboes or lumberjacks. We were not permitted to work at being sloppy."[5] For that reason and others he looked back upon his academy years with gratitude and pride.

In the fall of 1921, Kennan entered Princeton University, which Upton Sinclair was soon to dub "the first school of snobbishness in the United States."[6] He chose the Ivy League school in part because, as a senior at St. John's, he had read F. Scott Fitzgerald's newly published *This Side of Paradise*. Like Fitzgerald himself, the novel's protagonist, Amory Blaine, attends Princeton; like Kennan, he is from Wisconsin and, as Fitzgerald wrote, "he was unbearably lonely, desperately unhappy."[7]

Kennan's years at Princeton, where he majored in history, only deepened his feeling of isolation, of not belonging. "He found himself confronted," he wrote of his young self late in life, "with the greater sophistication and smoother manners of many of his fellow students and was brought to realize that he cut a very poor figure, if any at all, in their eyes."[8] He knew few of his peers and was known by fewer. He wept when, while still at Princeton, he read the passage in *The Great Gatsby* in which Nick Carraway speaks of his decision to leave the East and return to the Midwest. But unlike Nick, he found that he could not go home again; he decided—because his grades, even in history, were too low for admission to law school—to try for the newly organized foreign service.

To that end, he engaged a tutor to help him prepare for the exams, which he subsequently passed; and he began what was to become a legendary, though often difficult and controversial, career in the fall of 1926. In those days, Kennan later recalled, "there was a real old-fashioned dignity and simplicity about [the Department of State]. It was staffed . . . by professional personnel some of whom were men of great experience and competence."[9]

After several months at the Foreign Service School, Kennan was sent on temporary assignment to Geneva, where the Naval Disarmament Conference was in progress. As an official representative of the United States, he discovered that he could, and in order to perform his duties properly was obliged to, assume a new, less introverted, personality. But it was a mask, a way of overcoming, in public, an almost paralyzing self-consciousness. "Like the actor on the stage," he wrote in his memoirs, "I have been able, all my life, to be of greater usefulness to others by what, seen from a certain emotional distance, I seemed to be than by what, seen closely, I really was."[10] This confession is the key to understanding the apparent contradiction between the tough, cool political realist and man of the world and the sensitive, shy, introverted private person.

Toward the end of summer 1927, Kennan moved on to his first permanent post, at Hamburg. There, and for a few months in Berlin in 1928, he continued the project of creating a more extroverted public persona by immersing himself in the external world. He enrolled in evening classes offered by the city of Hamburg, watched with fascination a communist street demonstration, and adopted a new tack, inspired by Alfons Paquet, a travel writer able to discern deeper meanings behind surface realities, in the diaries he had already begun to keep.

In the preface to a selection of entries that he later published, Kennan observed that "the careful reader will perceive its [Paquet's travel book's] beneficent effects in the comparison between the juvenile entries from Hamburg of 1927, full of romantic preoccupation with self, written before Paquet's book was read, and the greater extroversion—the greater turning of the gaze outward—in the pieces written thereafter, in the Baltic countries and in Berlin."[11]

This did not mean that Kennan had lost interest in trying to understand himself; that he was never to lose. But he had now embarked upon a career in which excessive introversion would be a distinct handicap. Having thus turned his gaze outward, Kennan became acutely aware of the limits of his education; he therefore resolved to resign from the foreign service and to begin graduate studies. On arrival in Washington to submit his resignation, however, he had a chance encounter with William Dawson, chief of the Foreign Service School, who reminded him that he could receive training within the Service as a specialist in a little-known language—Chinese, Japanese, Arabic, or Russian. He chose Russian, in part because of what he took to be its future career promise, but also because of a family tradition begun by another George Kennan, born in 1845 on the same date as he, and a cousin of his grandfather.

That other George Kennan, a writer and lecturer from Norwalk, Ohio, set out for Siberia in the spring of 1885. Accompanying him was George A. Frost (the middle initial of our George Kennan stands for "Frost"), an artist and photographer from Boston. *Century Magazine* financed the journey, the purpose of which was to study at firsthand tsarist Russia's prison and exile systems. A former telegrapher, Kennan had made his first trip to Russia as a member of a team charged with advancing the project of linking America and Europe by a telegraph line that would run through Alaska, over the Bering Strait, and across Siberia to European Russia; the successful laying of the Atlantic Cable led to the project's abandonment.

Like Frost, Kennan spoke Russian and intended to confirm his belief that the tsar's government had received unjustified criticism for its treatment of revolutionaries, of whom he entertained a low opinion. During the difficult months that he and Frost traveled in Siberia, however, most of his "long-cherished opinions with regard to nihilists and the working of the exile system [were] completely overthrown."[12] The nihilists whom he met were not, he wrote in *Century Magazine* and later in *Siberia and the Exile System* (1891), crazy fanatics, but civilized, intelligent, and reasonable men and women. In view of the cruel and barbarous conditions to which they were subjected in exile, their resort to terrorism seemed not only unsurprising but perfectly defensible. Wrong a man with the utmost brutality, "deny him all redress, exile him again if he complains, gag him if he cries out, strike him in the face if he struggles, and at last he will stab and throw bombs."[13]

In his introduction to a reprint of *Siberia and the Exile System,* the later George Kennan painted a respectful portrait of his relative, but in a personally revealing passage he wondered about the absence of any published criticism of his character. This lacuna suggested that no one knew him well, no one "who could penetrate below the surface to the deeper reality of the human soul, which is never without weakness and contradiction."[14] He did not think that Kennan had taken full account "of the preposterous and indiscriminate campaign of terrorism" the revolutionaries had waged against the government and of the extent to which their criminal actions had provoked a response that fell upon them and others less guilty. He had come to think, in fact, that the tsarist government's treatment of revolutionaries had been, if anything, on the lenient side.

Kennan's observation concerning the ready reception which his relative's book and popular lectures received was also significant. "It was a time," he wrote, "when America was coming of age, abandoning the egocentricity of its youth, and turning its eyes to the world beyond its borders"—rather as he had done as he threw himself into his Russian studies. Before, however, he could begin those studies, Kennan had first to serve twelve to eighteen months in the Russian field, which, because the U.S. did not then maintain formal relations with the USSR, meant the Baltic states, only recently freed from Russian rule. In the summer of 1928, he took up an assignment as vice consul in Tallinn, Estonia, where he lived in solitude and began seriously to study Russian.

At the beginning of 1929, Kennan received a transfer to Riga, Latvia, where he served his "trial period" in preparation for training as a Russian specialist. But he also continued to keep a diary in order to perfect the art of writing. In an entry of March 29, 1929, he described a brief trip to Dorpat (now Tartu), Estonia. There he visited the ruins of an old cathedral, a sight that appealed to his melancholy temperament and his belief that he was alienated from his own era. "Even as a ruin," he wrote, the cathedral "becomes a towering reproach to the weakness of our own generation."[15]

That summer, Kennan moved on to Berlin where, for a year, he studied Russian subjects at the University of Berlin's Seminary for Oriental Languages, founded by the "Iron Chancellor," Otto von Bismarck. The following year he moved over to the university proper, where he took courses in Russian history from two distinguished professors: Otto Hoetsch and Karl Stählin.

This was the time of Christopher Isherwood's *Berlin Stories,* the years of the Depression and the rise of Adolf Hitler. But Kennan's world was not the cabaret world of "Mr. Ishevoo" and Sally Bowles. He lived quietly and, during his free time, regularly took up the pen. "Once," he later recalled, "I succeeded, with intense pride and excitement, in publishing an article in a liberal German magazine." His diary, however, remained his principal outlet. Those entries which he chose to publish reveal little concerning the Weimar Republic's death agony, though on August 8, 1931, he reported seeing a banner along the road to Stettin that read: "No one has any money. The French have taken everything from us."[16]

The destination of that particular journey was Norway, where Kennan was going to meet the parents of Annelise Soerensen, whom he had met in Berlin and to whom he was engaged. The two were married on September 11 and, after a honeymoon in Vienna, headed for Riga, where Kennan took up a new post in the Russian section of the American legation, one that he manned until autumn 1933. We know that he filled his diaries with travel accounts during those years, but he published only one, in the first volume of his memoirs; in it he wrote of his November 1932 visit to the port of Libau.

One cannot help but be struck by the young Kennan's powers of observation—sharpened no doubt by his habit of drawing sketches—and his sense, one that was to deepen over the years, of what Spengler, whom he had read with care, called *"Der Untergang des Abendlandes,"* the going under of the West. In Libau's factory district, he walked among the ruins of buildings. Will, he wondered, the buildings ever be brought back to life, or are they already museum pieces, "to be wondered at by future generations like the crooked medieval streets of Western European cities?"[17]

At his work desk, Kennan studied and reported on economic conditions in the USSR. Asked by a superior to provide an estimate of how the newly announced Five-Year Plan might affect public opinion, he produced a document, dated August 19, 1932, remarkable for its prescience. Great numbers of people, he pointed out, were discontented, their nerves shattered by the demands of rapid industrialization. Others, particularly the young, participated enthusiastically in a utopian project that made them forget the more personal questions of human existence.

At some point, however, one of two things would occur. Either the regime would achieve its economic goals and the young would begin to ask themselves what there was left to live for, or the plan would result in economic disappointment, even chaos, and the true believers would lose their faith and self-confidence. "From the most morally unified country in the world, Russia can become overnight the worst moral chaos."[18] In other words, Kennan foresaw the internal logic of the system and its ultimate collapse.

As impressive as Kennan's judgment was, he found his work to be something less than captivating, and in any event he wanted to write something other than official reports. During evenings and over weekends, he began to collect material for a literary biography of Anton Chekhov. Why Chekhov? Was it because the Russian playwright and master of the short story had, partly as a result of reading *Siberia and the Exile System,* made a fact-finding trip to Sakhalin Island? "From the books which I have read and am reading," Chekhov wrote to a friend before his departure in the spring of 1890, "it is clear that we have let millions of people rot in prison, have let them rot idly, without reasoning, barbarously."[19] In a devastating short story titled "In Exile," he explored the agonizing choice faced by exiles: either to forget their former life—wife, family, home—and thus avoid the pain of memory, or to cling to hope and thus live with heartbreak.

Perhaps what attracted Kennan was the famous objectivity that Chekhov perfected. In his memoirs, Kennan characterized the Russian's writings as "unparalleled . . . in perceptiveness, vividness, objectivity, and artistic feeling."[20] How better, he asked himself, to get a feel for prerevolutionary Russia? As a creative artist, Chekhov could reveal what it meant to live in tsarist times—meant at the profoundly personal level of existence.

For the Russian's ability to see through externals to the deeply personal, and to face reality without turning against life, Kennan felt the greatest admiration. As he later told a Princeton class, "no one, in any country or at any time, was more sensitive than he was—sensitive to cruelty, to brutality, to hypocrisy of every sort. Yet he never lost the love of life. To him, such things as beauty and laughter and conviviality and good food and the joy of creativity never paled." This was reflected in his stories, the essence of which was the mixture of tragedy and comedy.[21] Kennan read and reread Chekhov in order to learn creative writing from a master. He failed to complete the literary study he planned only because his wife presented him with their first child and his official duties absorbed much of his time.

Those duties were teaching him important, if unpalatable, truths about American statesmanship. In his memoirs, he told of a memorandum he drafted in the spring of 1933, warning that Soviet assurances concerning foreign nationals in Russia, even when formalized, would not in fact protect anyone from being arrested on charges of economic espionage. Washington ignored the warning because U.S. leaders cared less about the effect of their decisions—less about the national interest—than they did about how those decisions might appear to congressional and public opinion. One of the most incurable traits of American statesmanship, he concluded, was "its neurotic self-consciousness and introversion."[22] The choice of words is revealing.

Based upon his ever deepening knowledge of communist conduct, Kennan was not enthusiastic about President Roosevelt's decision to recognize the Soviet government, a decision that seems to have been motivated, at least in part, by fears concerning Japanese incursions into China and hopes of enlisting Russian help. Whatever his doubts about the wisdom of recognition, however, Kennan had prepared himself for service in Russia and was therefore pleased when the ambassador designate, William C. Bullitt, took him along as interpreter and aide when he traveled to Moscow to present his credentials.

Aboard the SS *President Harding,* which also carried *New York Times* correspondent Walter Duranty, whose denial of the Ukrainian famine of 1932–33 would eventually earn him infamy, Kennan and Bullitt became acquainted. Kennan later reported that he found the older man to be charming and confident, but also prideful and devoid of a sense of obligation to others; perhaps so, though he may have been reacting to the fact that, in the 1950s, Bullitt had accused him of trusting Soviet leaders and abandoning the peoples of Eastern Europe. Some years after Bullitt's death in 1967, Kennan sketched a verbal portrait of a man and a generation:

> I see Bill Bullitt, in retrospect, as a member of that re-
> markable group of young Americans, born just before the
> turn of the century (it included such people as Cole Porter,
> Ernest Hemingway, John Reed, and Jim Forrestal—many
> of them his friends) for whom the First World War was the
> great electrifying experience of life. They were a striking
> generation, full of talent and exuberance, determined—if
> one may put it so—to make life come alive. The mark
> they made on American culture will be there when many
> other marks have faded. But in most of them there seems
> to have been a touch of the fate, if not the person, of the
> Great Gatsby.[23]

These people knew, Kennan concluded, achievement more often than fulfillment. That was certainly true of Bullitt, who by the time of his appointment had gone through two marriages, the second to the bohemian widow of John Reed, Louise Bryant. Bullitt arrived in Stalin's Russia with high hopes and left, profoundly disillusioned, three years later. Kennan did not suffer a similar disillusionment because he never had any illusions to begin with. "Never," he wrote in his memoirs, "did I consider the Soviet Union a fit ally or associate, actual or potential, for this country."[24] This view could only be reinforced by the experience of living in Moscow at the time of the purges, an experience made no easier when Joseph E. Davies, a "useful idiot" married to General Foods heiress Marjorie Merriweather Post, replaced Bullitt.

In *Mission to Moscow,* a "classic" of its kind, Davies wrote that the Great Terror's "trials, purges and liquidations, which seemed so violent at the time and shocked the world, are now [1941] quite clearly a part of a . . . determined effort of the Stalin government to protect itself from not only revolution from within but from attack from without. They went to work thoroughly to clear up and clean out all treasonable elements within the country. All doubts were resolved in favor of the government."[25]

Not in Kennan's view. As Davies's interpreter, he attended the Second Moscow Trial (January 1937)—of the so-called "Anti-Soviet Trotskyite Center." In the dock were seventeen men, most notably Yuri Pyatakov, an economic administrator who had played a pivotal role in the industrialization of the USSR but who had sided with Trotsky in the struggle to succeed Lenin; and Karl Radek, a Bolshevik intellectual well known in the West. Many of the others were shabby characters, included in order to create the impression that the prominent figures were themselves shabby and low. According to the indictment, members of the Center planned to sabotage industry, restore capitalism, spy for the Germans and Japanese, and assassinate Soviet leaders. To the surprise of no one, every defendant confessed his guilt; Radek did so with such apparent relish that he escaped the death penalty—though he was killed in prison in 1939.

Pyatakov, who must have known that he was a dead man, made a last, pathetic, plea. "In a few hours you will pass your sentence. And here I stand before you in filth, crushed by my own crimes, bereft of everything through my own fault, a man who has lost his Party, who has no friends, who has lost his family, who has lost his very self."[26] Kennan recalled that one "could see [the defendants] there, and their pale faces, their twitching lips, their evasive eyes. These were the faces of men who had been, if not tortured, then terrified in many ways and often by threats to take it out on their families if they didn't confess. But they had been through hell, and they knew that these were likely to be their last hours."[27] At the time, he discerned another reason for the Purge victims' willingness to confess, one that anticipated Arthur Koestler's famous theory in *Darkness at Noon* (1941), a novel of the trials: "[Sergei] Mrachkovski and [N. I.] Muralov [confessed] because they were sincere fanatical old Bolsheviks and had been convinced by their jailors that they owed it to the Revolution to do this."[28]

As always, Kennan was most content when committing his thoughts to paper. In an unofficial essay titled "The War Problem of the Soviet Union," he described Stalin's military build-up and cynical attitude toward treaty obligations. The Soviet Union, he argued, sought not to avoid war but to postpone it until prospects were most favorable. Even then, it would make every effort to avoid serious risk and, after others exhausted themselves, claim the spoils. Such pessimism with respect to Soviet intentions and Soviet-American relations was, he knew, a far cry from the almost criminal pro-Soviet attitude of Davies and the excessively sunny outlook of FDR himself.

One of the ways in which Kennan learned to release his frustration was to read—especially chapters in Edward Gibbon's great *History of the Decline and Fall of the Roman Empire*. Another was to travel and record his impressions. Still interested in Chekhov, he made pilgrimages to places where the Russian writer had lived—Babkino and Voskresensk. To his considerable regret, the locals could—or would—pass on little concerning the famous writer. And on his return to work, Kennan was still subject to Davies's authority. He was therefore relieved when, in mid-1937, Washington appointed him Consul in Jerusalem and then, before he could set out for Palestine, summoned him home to take over the Russian desk in the State Department's Division of European Affairs. He would serve in that capacity for a year, during which he discovered important truths about himself and about his relationship to his country— witness his diary account of a June 1938 bicycle trip across his native Wisconsin.

In that account he reflected upon American individualism, which in his view had all but destroyed any sense of community, any instinct for human association. Automobiles—he called them "machines"—raced along highways at such speeds that travelers lost all meaningful connection with the land and those who remained close to the land. In farm dwellers, the machines only deepened the feeling of loneliness. He found himself wishing, as Chekhov had wished with regard to the evils of his Russia, that some cataclysm "would carry away something of this stuffy individualism and force human beings to seek their happiness and their salvation in their relationship to society as a whole rather than in the interests of themselves and their little group of intimate acquaintances."[29]

As this reflection suggests, and as Kennan made clear in his memoirs, he felt estranged from the land of his birth. "Increasingly," he later confessed, "I would not be a part of my country, although what it had once been would remain a part of me." As a matter of self-respect, he would continue to pledge his loyalty, but it would be "a loyalty of principle, not of identification."[30] In the midst of war shadows, the Depression, the New Deal, and calls for even more radical change, Kennan began to write a prescription of his own: he titled it "The Prerequisites: Notes on Problems of the United States in 1938." As shocking to Americans as it would have seemed, had it been published (no doubt he thought the medicine too strong for his countrymen), the treatise advanced ideas that Kennan was later to modify but not wholly repudiate.

Although he thought well of the Constitution as originally drafted, he argued that later generations had perverted "what was supposed to be a representative government into a boss ridden democracy." He recognized that this unfortunate transformation could be attributed largely to the country's acceptance of universal suffrage. "It is obvious," he wrote, "that there are millions of people in this country who haven't the faintest conception of the rights or wrongs of the complicated questions with which the federal government is faced."[31] In response to this truth, he called for the disenfranchisement of naturalized citizens, women, and blacks. Such an idea would outrage twenty-first century sensibilities, and one could easily cite reasons to oppose blanket disenfranchisements. But the principle of a franchise limited not by sex or color but by education, property ownership, and tax assessments is no more arbitrary and unreasonable now than it was in the eighteenth century.

Limitation of the franchise was, Kennan continued, but one step "along a road which very few Americans are willing to contemplate: along the road which leads through constitutional change to the authoritarian state."[32] He had in mind the Austrian government of Kurt von Schuschnigg, which had only recently fallen victim to the Anschluss. He had been in Vienna in 1935 while recuperating from a bout with ulcers and had admired the manner in which the government, drawing upon the advice of experts rather than of members of Parliament or the populace, went about its business.

It was on this matter, government by a well-prepared elite rather than by "The People," that Kennan focused his attention. His idea was similar to that advanced by Plato in the *Republic*. An elite group of men ought to be identified and trained for government service—they "would have to subject themselves to discipline as they would if they entered a religious order."[33] This was, Kennan believed, the only way in which government could be placed on a secure footing. As the years went by, however, he saw not only the utter rejection of his vision but the irreversible triumph of its very opposite: a vulgar populism manipulated by an incompetent, corrupt, and self-aggrandizing elite.

Kennan's alienation was therefore destined to grow, and it was with a deepening pessimism concerning his country that, in September 1938, he set out for Prague, where a new and challenging assignment awaited him; he arrived in the Czech capital on September 29, the day that the infamous Munich Conference opened. In Hitler's "Brown House," Britain and France quickly agreed that Czechoslovakia should cede to Germany those areas of predominantly German-speaking population that rimmed the "Historic Provinces" of Bohemia and Moravia. At no time, according to Hitler's translator, Paul Schmidt, did Prime Minister Chamberlain believe the Führer's demands to be unreasonable[34]—even though the redrawing of the Czech frontiers carried with it serious military implications. The Czechs' formidable frontier defenses were to be taken over by the Germans.

Seeing that Czechoslovakia had been abandoned by the Western powers, Poland occupied Teschen, and Hungary occupied the southern rim of Slovakia and the southwest corner of Ruthenia, areas it had ruled prior to 1914. As Second Secretary of the American Legation, Kennan's principal duty was political reporting. He could not have been more pleased, because this task provided him with an opportunity to sharpen his powers of observation and to perfect the art of writing. "I wrote with pleasure and enthusiasm," he later recalled, "aware that I was gradually mastering the complexities of the situation and was writing better than I had ever written before."[35]

Hostile to imperialism of any kind, Kennan deplored Hitler's aggression, but unlike many in the West, he did not think of Czechoslovakia as a model of political virtue. Of the much-lauded Czech democracy he had this to say in a private paper: "[I was] unable to share that enthusiasm for democracy in Czechoslovakia that seemed almost an obsession to so many Anglo-Saxon liberals."[36] Moreover, he believed Czech nationalism to be another example of that individualism that had so corrupted his own country. He saw too that the fragmentation of power in Central Europe that resulted from the Great War was a recipe for disaster. In "personal notes" made in October 1938, shortly after Munich, he wrote that "it is generally agreed that the breakup of the limited degree of unity which the Hapsburg Empire represented was unfortunate for all concerned."[37]

About the "general agreement," Kennan may have been mistaken, but he was right about the destruction of Austria-Hungary. Of all the ill-considered decisions the peacemakers made, that one was the most foolhardy and damaging; with the exception of Poland and Hungary, none of the successor states could get along with any other. Even within what were supposed to be ethnic states, ethnic minorities were many, and ethnic rivalries rose to the level of hatreds—nowhere more so than in multi-ethnic Czechoslovakia, or as the Slovaks preferred, "Czecho-Slovakia." Caught between two temporarily weakened and pariah Great Powers, the unhappy fate of the successor states should have been predictable.

Far better than most, Kennan recognized this geopolitical fact. At the same time, he was cautiously optimistic about the Czechs' future because he believed in the futility of any effort by one people to ride roughshod over the national feelings of another, particularly in the circumstances of the modern age. Because of this conviction, he opposed what he characterized as the "romanticism" of hopeless resistance and counseled the admittedly humiliating "but truly heroic [solution] of realism."[38] To him, the limited collaboration of the beleaguered Czech president Emil Hácha was preferable to suicidal resistance.

Nor did he change his mind when, on March 15, 1939, Hitler sent his troops into Bohemia and Moravia and established a "protectorate." To complete the destruction of Czechoslovakia, the Führer allowed Slovakia to declare its (nominal) independence and handed what was left of Ruthenia over to Hungary. Kennan stayed on in Prague as an officer charged with maintaining custody of U.S. diplomatic files and preserving U.S. property. As was his custom, he took long walks so that he could observe daily life and reflect upon the reality with which the Czechs were confronted.

Technically, the Hácha government still existed, and, at least at first, daily life changed very little. As a result, many Czechs appeared to lapse into "Schweikism," a kind of sly submission to authority. The word derives from the behavior of the "good soldier Schweik," antihero of a World War I novel by the Czech author Jaroslav Hašek; it is not meant to be flattering. Nevertheless, in Kennan's view, anything that maintained some continuity of life and that held out promise, however small, for the future was better than a reckless effort to seek martyrdom, or to be more precise, national annihilation.

This was a hard doctrine; it stemmed not from any want of courage or faintness of heart, but rather from a deep conviction that one had to accept the world as it was, not as one might wish it to be. Perhaps because he recognized in himself a personal weakness for romanticism, Kennan pressed all the more for a public realism. The government papers that he prepared in Prague are strikingly detached. One suspects that what Desmond MacCarthy once wrote of Henry James could also be said of Kennan: "There is a kind of detachment (it is to be felt in the deeply religious, in some artists, in some imaginative men of action), which seems to bring the possessor of it at once nearer to his fellow beings than others get, and at the same time to remove him into a kind of solitude."[39] His cool, and as it turned out overly optimistic, reports concerning the plight of the Jews, particularly those in Slovakia, are cases in point.

But one should also consider Kennan's personal writings. In a letter to his wife, dated October 21, 1941, he reported that

> in general, life in Berlin has been much as you knew it. The major change has been the wearing of the star by the Jews. That is a fantastically barbaric thing. I shall never forget the faces of people in the subway with the great yellow star sewed onto their overcoats, standing, not daring to sit down or to brush against anybody, staring straight ahead of them with eyes like terrified beasts—nor the sight of little children running around with those badges sewn on them.[40]

In a letter he wrote to his sister during a brief fact-finding trip to Prague (from Berlin) in December 1940, Kennan spoke of feeling in the marrow of his bones "the incorrigible vanity and tragedy and futility of all human endeavor."[41] Each generation, he had come to believe, deludes itself by thinking that what it has done will last—and the works of each are swept away. The more Kennan was assailed by such somber reflections, the more he sought solace in writing. "When I am in Prague," he told his sister, "I simply have to write. . . . I have written so many formal things about this part of the world that I think I have paid my due to literary discipline and decorum and am entitled to indulge once in the 'stream of consciousness' stuff."[42]

By the time Kennan wrote the letter, Hitler had launched World War II in Europe by invading Poland. The Department of State therefore transferred their man from Prague to Berlin, where he was to continue in his reporting role. This assignment he was prepared to accept, but on arrival in the German capital he discovered that he would also have to assume administrative burdens, not only on behalf of U.S. interests but of those of much of the Western world. This he did, while at the same time trying to gauge how far Germans identified themselves with the Nazi regime's objectives. He concluded that for most, the war was Hitler's, not theirs. Going against the American grain, as he almost always did, he could not regard the German people as inhuman monsters who were solidly behind Hitler and consumed with a demonic determination to enslave the rest of Europe.

That, however, was precisely how President Roosevelt regarded them. After America's entry into the war, FDR turned a deaf ear to all appeals for support emanating from the camp of German resistance. Despite repeated entreaties from "Wild Bill" Donovan, director of the Office of Strategic Services (OSS), and Allen Dulles, who ran intelligence operations out of Switzerland, the president refused to provide support or encouragement of any kind. To make matters worse, he proclaimed the Allied policy of "unconditional surrender" at Casablanca on January 13, 1943. The policy dealt a devastating blow to the resistance's morale and undermined all efforts to overthrow Hitler and establish a new government. At the same time, it contributed to the lengthening of the war and the consequent death of millions, very much including Europe's Jews.

FDR's Germanophobia was a result not only of World War I propaganda concerning the "Hun," but also of his contempt for conservatives and aristocrats, labels that described most of the resistance leaders. He had no intention, he told Donovan, of giving aid to the "vons"; Americans were fighting and dying for democracy, not aristocracy.[43] For such an attitude, Kennan had no sympathy whatever. In a letter to Sir Ernest Llewellyn Woodward of March 1965, he called attention to the great imbalance between Allied abhorrence of Hitler and "the very low value" placed upon "the willingness of other Germans to accept the enormous risks of trying to overthrow him."[44]

There is no doubt that Kennan's view of this matter was greatly influenced by his clandestine contacts with members of the German opposition, in particular Gottfried Bismarck, grandson of the great chancellor, and Count Helmuth von Moltke, a great-grandnephew of the legendary field marshal. Moltke, who was serving military intelligence as an advisor concerning international law, was a pivotal figure in the resistance as the leader of the Kreisau Circle, named by the Gestapo after the Moltke family estate in Silesia. Like Kennan, he had a strong aversion to violent means, whatever the projected ends. Having been raised a Christian Scientist, he had lost his faith but did embrace a kind of moralizing Protestantism during the years that he worked against the Nazi regime. He possessed, according to Kennan, "a vision of Christianity broad, tolerant, and all-embracing, like that of Pasternak, in the range of its charity."[45]

Moltke was a profoundly conservative man, and precisely for that reason he welcomed into his circle a number of undogmatic socialists who, like him, believed that Germany would have to drink the full cup of defeat before it could begin to renew its moral and spiritual life. His was above all a civilizational resistance to a barbarism that could not be uprooted simply by assassinating Hitler, something he opposed as a matter of principle in any case. For him, as the late German historian Joachim Fest pointed out, mass society was the great scourge of the time;[46] he was appalled by egalitarianism and favored an authoritarianism disciplined by Christian moral principles. Arrested by the Gestapo on January 19, 1944, this great and courageous man was hanged in Plötzensee prison on January 23, 1945. "Some day," Kennan wrote in a letter of 1962, "he should take his place among the great Protestant Christian martyrs, for it was really religious conviction which carried him along a path he himself knew would probably lead him to his death."[47]

Moltke exerted a deep and lasting influence on Kennan. In his memoirs, the American wrote that the martyred German "has remained for me over the intervening years a pillar of moral conscience and an unfailing source of political and intellectual inspiration."[48] He reinforced Kennan's principled opposition to mass democracy and his admiration for an old-fashioned authoritarianism that, unlike totalitarianism, maintained order without destroying liberty or imposing a political religion. As it was for Moltke, the past was for Kennan preferable to the modern world. While in wartime Berlin, Kennan prepared a position paper for Under Secretary of State Sumner Welles, who had been sent to Europe by President Roosevelt to sound out political leaders concerning the possibility of a negotiated peace. He concluded by recommending a postwar partition of Germany and "a return to the particularism of the eighteenth century—a return to the small kingdoms, the chocolate soldiers, the picturesque localisms of an earlier day."[49]

Kennan must have known that this was wildly unrealistic, but it testifies to a cast of mind. More realistic was his deepening conviction that even if the Nazis were to achieve a complete military victory in Europe, they would never succeed in solving the twin problems of political organization and control. There was nothing, Gibbon had written, "more contrary to nature than the attempt to hold in obedience distant provinces."[50] Based upon later Soviet attempts to dominate Eastern Europe, this has proved true, and it is characteristic of the historically informed, long-term view that Kennan never abandoned. Rather than taking incalculable risks, particularly after the dawn of the atomic age, Kennan almost always preferred to play a waiting game.

This did not mean, of course, that he harbored the slightest sympathy for the "Soviet experiment," as admirers were pleased to call it. On June 24, 1941, two days after Hitler ordered his troops into Russia, Kennan wrote a personal note to Loy Henderson, then a deputy chief of the State Department's Division of European Affairs. It was remarkable for its realistic assessment and its determination not to be moved by contemporary enthusiasms. He told Henderson that he did not think it wise or prudent to extend moral support to the besieged Soviets. Unlike those with short memories, he remembered that the USSR had been an imperialistic ally of Nazi Germany for almost two years. Russian involvement in the struggle against Hitler was thrust upon it by the June 22 attack. He did not rule out the extension of material aid, should it serve vital American interests, but he strongly advised against any close identification with the Russian war effort.

Only a few months after Kennan had advanced these views, the Japanese attacked Pearl Harbor. Four days later, Hitler declared war on the United States and ordered the Gestapo to take American embassy personnel, Kennan included, into custody. On December 14, 1941, he and 113 other Americans, seventeen of whom were journalists, were herded onto a train bound for Bad Nauheim, near Frankfurt. For the next five months, the Germans, under the command of an SS officer, held them incommunicado in Jeschke's Grand Hotel, which had been closed since the outbreak of war; it was therefore very far from being in peak condition.

Although Leland Morris, the embassy's chargé d'affairs, was among the internees, he preferred that Kennan assume responsibility for the disciplinary control that would be necessary. This was a thankless task, as Kennan knew it would be. His fellow internees' "cares, their quarrels, their jealousies, their complaints," he later recalled, "filled every moment of my waking day."[51] He was, however, the man best suited to exercise authority. Perfectly aware that democracy would work no better in the Grand Hotel than it did elsewhere, he created a "secretariat" to establish rules of conduct, draw up duty rosters, receive complaints, and deal with the Germans.

Above all, the secretariat implemented the decision to cooperate with the internees' captors, this in an effort to maximize their personal liberty. The hardships with which Kennan and his charges had to deal included poor food, lack of heat, boredom, and the tensions arising from living in close quarters, under guard, with relative strangers. These were made worse by the uncertainty surrounding their fate. They received no word from their own government, which could have communicated with them through the Swiss representatives who sometimes visited. Some began to fear that they would remain prisoners until the war ended.

It was important for order and morale that activities be organized. One of the most successful was the "Badheim University," created by Phillip Whitcomb, a former Rhodes Scholar who had been Associated Press correspondent in Paris. After conducting a survey of the intellectual talent on hand, he scheduled classes on a wide range of subjects: languages, phonetics, civics, Bible study, physical education, tap dancing, philosophy, and Russian history.[52] In offering the latter course, Kennan launched an illustrious, if intermittent, teaching career.

Those who attended his lectures must have been aware that there stood before them a gifted teacher who possessed a complete mastery of his subject and a rare ability to express himself clearly and eloquently. Climate and geography, he declared in one lecture, were major factors in the making of the Russian nation. The vastness of the countryside had given the Russians a sense of infinite possibility and created in them a tendency to extremism. People who lived on islands or in mountain valleys were more apt to develop a sense of restraint and moderation, to recognize the limitations to which all human beings were subject.

Like many historians, Kennan placed emphasis upon the legacy of the Mongol period in Russian history, c. 1240–1480. From the khan and his rule, he argued, Russians inherited habits of disloyalty and cruelty and the practice of humiliating prominent figures publicly—as Stalin did during the purges. Fortunately, another factor, the Orthodox Church, mitigated this inheritance. Throughout the period of Mongol rule the church carried on its activities, "caring for the souls of individual people, helping them over the agonies of birth and death, building monasteries in the great forests, cultivating and preserving the scanty arts . . . providing shelters for the lonely, the weak, the sick, the sensitive, for all those, in short, who could not stomach the crudeness and bestiality of the day."[53] It was, Kennan concluded, this spiritual resistance and resilience that would carry Russians through the trials and sufferings of later centuries.

In another lecture, Kennan called his listeners' attention to the striking parallels between Russian and American history. In both lands, he said, European culture of the eighteenth century planted deep roots. It was, in fact, that culture "for which," Kennan said in a personal aside, "many old-fashioned Americans still have so deep a nostalgia: the dignity, the severe simplicity, the deep respect for form, the polished, classical erudition, the easy acceptance of a clear stratification of society." It is important to note that in this connection he referred especially to the American South. In both Russia and America, he concluded sadly, industrialism had destroyed that culture, leading their peoples "from the order and clarity and security" of the eighteenth century into "the tossing chaos" of the twentieth.[54]

Kennan's lectures broke off in the middle of the reign of Alexander I (1801–25), because in April 1942, he and the others received word that they were to be exchanged for German internees in the United States. On May 12, they boarded a train that carried them to Lisbon, where the Swedish ship *Drottning-holm* awaited them. Kennan was greatly relieved to be free of the heavy, and not very pleasant, burdens he had borne with his customary dignity and sense of duty. He had learned much, he later reflected, about human beings in adversity. "I came away with a new admiration for one portion of mankind, but a portion which, as I now recognized, would never be more than a minority."[55] He looked forward to a much-needed rest, and on his arrival home he and his wife used the time to search for and purchase their first home, a 235-acre farm in the family tradition. It was located in East Berlin, Pennsylvania, some twenty miles from the Eisenhower farm.

Just before Labor Day, Kennan received orders to proceed to neutral Portugal, where he was to be counselor of legation—though secretly he was also to coordinate U.S. intelligence operations in the country. In his new role he expended much of his energy in an effort to secure U.S. use of naval ports and air landings in the Azores, nine major islands extending some five hundred miles in the Atlantic. Much energy was needed because of his own government's imperious attitude toward Portuguese interests and sovereignty, jealously guarded by Prime Minister António de Oliveira Salazar. Of Salazar, Kennan quickly formed a favorable opinion. "I am convinced," he wrote in an official letter of December 11, 1944, that "Salazar, operating on a set of principles which are quite different from our own principles of democracy, has created and maintained conditions of life far more credible and acceptable to the psychology of the people than the conditions which prevailed there under a theoretically democratic and republican form of government prior to his advent to power."[56]

Although Kennan obtained Salazar's agreement, he was recalled to Washington before he could finalize arrangements. His next stop was London, where he was to act as political advisor to Ambassador John G. Winant, the American delegate to the newly established European Advisory Commission. The commission, made up of U.S., British, and Russian delegates, was to begin preparations for a unified approach to the problems of a postwar Germany. FDR did not wish, however, to have his hands tied, and, there being little for Winant to do, Kennan returned to the U.S. in the spring of 1944. Although his advice was never sought, he had very decided views concerning Germany. In part they were dictated by his Germanophilia, in part by his clear-eyed awareness of the threat posed by the Soviet Union.

In a memorandum he wrote in Washington late in 1943 before setting out for London, Kennan stated his objections to government plans to bar anyone suspected of undemocratic sympathies from active participation in the making of a new Germany. In the first place, in his view, the plan was impractical—it would be impossible, without committing injustices and stirring resentment, to identify, without error, those who might prove untrustworthy. Second, it was going to be difficult enough, if not impossible, to find enough people competent to assume administrative burdens. Finally, the elimination of "nationalist elements" was unnecessary, the war having taught them a lesson they would not soon forget.

This was wise counsel, but as Kennan later made clear it was rooted in his belief that, by allying themselves with Moscow, the Americans and British had tacitly accepted a brutal manner of warfare that was not peculiar to the Germans. "In judging the individual cruelties of this struggle," he made bold to assert, history "will not distinguish between those of victor and vanquished."[57] Because the U.S. would have to associate itself with the USSR in judging and punishing German conduct, he opposed any large-scale program of "denazification."

Kennan did not disguise the fact that his views on policy toward the Soviet Union were at odds with those of FDR, of whom he had formed an unfavorable opinion, and other administration leaders, even when Averell Harriman, then the U.S. ambassador in Moscow, asked him to serve as the embassy's minister-counselor. If Harriman was put off by Kennan's stance, he did not show it, because he needed someone with his experience and linguistic competence. In early June 1944, therefore, Kennan left Washington. He made a stopover in Lisbon, where his family was staying temporarily, and used the time to warn his fellow foreign service officers that life would not be easy in postwar America "if we are going to defend successfully . . . the things most of us were taught to feel as children; things like independence of speech and thought, honesty and courage of public life, dignity and quiet serenity of the home and of the family."[58]

One of Kennan's next stopovers was in Baghdad, where he found, among other unattractive things, religious bigotry and a fanaticism that kept women "confined and excluded from the productive efforts of society by a system of indefinite house arrest." He thought then, as he thought later, that the United States would be wise to avoid assuming any responsibility for improving the depressing state of Middle Eastern affairs. For one thing, the U.S. was incapable of pursuing a long-term and consistent policy in an area so remote from its own territory. For another, it had business to take care of at home. Americans should "restrain their excitement at the silent, expectant possibilities in the Middle Eastern deserts, and . . . return, like disappointed but dutiful children, to the sad deficiencies and problems of their native land."[59] Sound and prudent advice it was.

From Baghdad, Kennan flew to Tehran, where he waited for a visa that would allow him to reenter Russia. It soon was granted. He then flew to Moscow, arriving on July 1, 1944. During his two-year assignment in the Soviet capital, he became fully conscious, if he had not been before, of the fact that he was, before anything else, a writer. He knew that Chekhov had famously described medicine as his wife, literature as his mistress; he now came to the conclusion that diplomacy was *his* wife, writing his mistress. That he preferred to spend time with his "mistress" is demonstrated not only by the fact that he was so often at odds with official Washington, but that he gave so much of himself to his writing, official and personal, and labored with such determination to perfect his style.

Of the many problems that Kennan and his colleagues faced in mid-1944, the most pressing was that of Poland. In pursuance of their "Nonaggression Pact" of 1939, Nazi Germany and Soviet Russia shared in the partitioning of Polish territory. The Polish government-in-exile, established in London, could never, of course, recognize the legitimacy of that partition. When

Hitler turned on Stalin in the summer of 1941, the Soviet tyrant, under pressure from his new allies, agreed to recognize the London government. He refused, however, to agree to restore to Poland those territories which the Red Army had taken when acting in concert with the Nazi dictator.

Furthermore, it did not take Stalin long to begin to undermine the Polish government he had just recognized. On Soviet territory, he set up a committee of Polish communists to rival the London government. Matters came to a head when, in the spring of 1943, the Germans discovered the mass graves of some five thousand Polish officers, murdered by the Soviets in the Katyn Forest. Stalin accused the Germans of the murders and broke off relations with the London government, which had demanded an investigation by the International Red Cross.

It was at that moment that Kennan, not yet returned to Russia, recognized that Stalin was determined to install a communist regime in Poland at war's end—not so much because he wanted a "friendly government" to his west, but because he could not tolerate a government that would investigate Soviet war crimes. He therefore resigned himself to the fact that Stanislaw Mikolajczyk, the London premier, would never play a role in postwar Poland. What was the point, then, of sending him, as Roosevelt and Churchill did, to Moscow to reason with Stalin?

Before poor Mikolajczyk left Moscow, where he achieved nothing, the Warsaw uprising began. It took the Germans sixty-three days to subdue the rebels, while the Red Army stood idly by; Stalin wanted to see the most independent and courageous Poles dead—so much so that he refused to allow the U.S. the use of military airfields it maintained in Ukraine for operations in support of the Polish fighters. The Soviet mask was now completely removed. Kennan believed then, as later, that the Western Allies should not pretend that the wartime alliance was anything other than it was: not even a marriage, but an affair of convenience.

Soviet territory had been liberated; why should the U.S. and the West continue to aid Stalin or to assume responsibility for the Soviet conquest of non-Soviet territory? Why, moreover, should the U.S. in particular continue to court Stalin in the vain hope of extending the wartime collaboration by erecting international organizations that were likely to deceive an uninformed public into believing that peace and cooperation could be brought about by the publication of documents studded with the language of Western liberal idealism, a language to which the Soviet Union assigned its own peculiar meanings?

In a paper dated August 4, 1944—and meant only to clarify his own thinking—Kennan observed that "an international organization for preservation of the peace and security cannot take the place of a well-conceived and realistic foreign policy."[60] While he had no objection to efforts to encourage the rule of law in international life, he maintained that for the foreseeable future, power would always trump law. To pretend otherwise was to invite misunderstanding and court disaster. Hence, he opposed the establishment of the United Nations.

Clearly, Kennan was becoming increasingly uneasy about his government's attitude toward the coming postwar period, particularly its illusions concerning Stalin and the Soviet Union. "Conscience," he wrote in his memoirs, "forced me to attempt to reduce to words on paper the view I held of the nature of the Soviet leaders and of the situation in which they found themselves as they entered upon this final phase of the war."[61] Completed in September 1944, "Russia—Seven Years Later" was, Kennan said late in his life, basic to an understanding of many of his subsequent papers.

And so it was. In it he cast Stalin, though a Georgian by birth, as the new Ivan the Terrible and Peter the Great, a man pitilessly realistic and determined to protect his personal power by increasing that of Russia. After the war, Kennan believed, the Soviet dictator would continue along the road of military industrialization and insist upon Russian control of Central and Eastern Europe. He would care little about world revolution but greatly about Soviet power and the uses of foreign fellow travelers. They, he concluded, would help to convince naïve Westerners that the wartime era of good feelings could and should continue, any diminution being a result of Western insensitivity to Russia's legitimate interests.

As usual, Kennan took a far kinder view of the Russian people. While they were in no position to disobey Soviet authorities or to express discontent, they had erected a fence around their "souls." The deepest recesses of their being could not be intruded upon. Thus the future was not without hope. Even the lack of consumer goods and amusements had its upside. "In contrast to our restless city dwellers," Kennan wrote, the Russians "can still take time to look at the earth and sky, to take note of the passage of the seasons, to sit quietly on a bench on a summer evening, to rest, to dream."[62]

These simple pleasures of life were those which meant most to Kennan himself, those he found missing in his own country and in the Western world in general. Their absence, as he believed, was one of the things that made him a stranger in the land of his birth, a lonely and isolated figure. But his loneliness was not only personal; it was professional as well. In the moving final sentences of his long paper, Kennan observed that while there would, in America, be much talk of "understanding Russia," there would be no place for someone like him who made a serious attempt to do just that. "The best he can look forward to is the lonely pleasure of one who stands at long last on a chilly and inhospitable mountaintop where few have been before, where few can follow, and where few will consent to believe that he has been."[63]

Kennan gave his paper to his chief, Ambassador Harriman, who said of it not a word. This lack of response wounded him, but not, significantly enough, because he thought his boss owed him comments on the paper's political content. "I did think," he confessed in his memoirs, "he might have observed, if he thought so, that it was well written. I personally felt, as I finished it, that I was making progress, technically and stylistically, in the curious art of writing for one's self alone. But I would have welcomed reassurance"—particularly from someone whom he respected and liked, despite the fact that, in contrast to himself, Harriman "regarded himself more as an operator than as an observer."[64]

When the war in Europe ended in May 1945, Kennan could not be counted among those for whom euphoria was the dominant emotion. He foresaw serious postwar problems with the Russians and warned that the Allied Control Commission (ACC), on which the British and Americans had only observer status, was an instrument of Soviet policy; he therefore recommended withdrawal. Association with the commission had already misled public opinion in the U.S. and saddled the government with a share of responsibility for policies that had nothing to do with America's ideals or interests.

At about the same time, he penned a long reflection titled "Russia's International Position at the Close of the War with Germany." As always, he took pains to say what he had to say with as much literary grace as he was able to muster. The postwar period, he warned, would pose real dangers to the West; steady nerves would be required. Western leaders would have to remember that Russia's wartime expansion into East-Central Europe had little if anything to do with the appeal of Marxism and much to do with the country's traditional geopolitical ambitions—it was a replay of the tsars' western expansion in the eighteenth and nineteenth centuries.

As usual, Kennan played the former century off against the latter. "As long," he wrote, "as the eighteenth-century principles of tolerance and good form were observed, even Poland did not seem to cause much trouble. But the nineteenth century, with its abolition of serfdom, its industrialism, and its attempts at Russification, made of the western provinces a hotbed out of which there grew the greater part of the Russian Social Democratic Party which bore Lenin to power."[65] The Soviet Union, he argued, was very likely to be confronted by a similar hostility. As a result, the burden of imperial rule would eventually prove to be too great. If the United States and other Western powers resisted the temptation—presented by excessive hopes for Russian-Western cooperation—to provide the Soviet Union with moral and material assistance and pursued a firm balance-of-power policy, the latter would soon discover that it had bitten off more than it could chew.

Kennan did not believe that Western resolve in the face of Russian provocation would lead the world into a new war. Stalin was a brutal dictator but he was not a reckless adventurer. A realist, he would not respond to Western steadfastness by unleashing an armed conflict that could well result in his own fall from power; in this judgment, we now know, Kennan was right—just as he was about Eastern Europe. In 1948, Tito's Yugoslavia broke with the Soviet Bloc, and after Stalin's death in 1953 Eastern European resistance stiffened, with the Hungarian Revolution of 1956 standing as the defining event in the history of the Russian occupation. To the peoples of the region, of course, the occupation seemed endless, but from the point of view of the West, and of history, it was mercifully brief; and without a shooting war, the occupation did collapse under its own weight.

Kennan was able to present his ideas clearly and gracefully, but he knew that position papers offered only limited possibilities for the perfection of a writing style. Then, too, they gave scope only to his *public* persona. A month after he had written "Russia's International Position," he was delighted to receive long-delayed permission from the Soviet authorities to visit major cities in Siberia. The journey was consistent with his duties as the number two man at the embassy, but the real reasons for his going were his desire to follow in the footsteps of his forebear and namesake and to use the opportunity to record on paper some reflections—a "literary account," he later called it.[66]

That account, published many years later, witnesses to Kennan's conscious effort to discover his true self in more personal prose. Among the things he learned about himself was that, however much he despised the Soviet regime, he continued to possess a profound admiration for the Russian people. "Here," he concluded, "was indubitably one of the world's greatest peoples." They had known the kind of suffering and struggles that Americans could scarcely imagine, but as a result they had been purged "of so much that is vulgar and inane in the softer civilizations."[67] He thought then, as he thought later, that their suffering had made them particularly sensitive to the great and perennial issues of human existence.

Of the regime's essential character he had no doubt; hence, he thought it best if the United States recognize the reality, though not the justice, of the division of postwar Europe into Western and Soviet spheres of influence. Any hope that Eastern European governments would be anything other than Stalinist in nature was delusional; it would be wise, therefore, to focus efforts on rebuilding Western Europe, where the United States retained some freedom of action. About the eastern half of the continent, nothing, at least for the moment, could be done. In fact, Kennan was coming around to the view that, as a rule, one country could do little to alter conditions in another (particularly a tyranny).

This view and others, including skepticism concerning the ability of democracies to conduct a mature, realistic foreign policy, guaranteed that Kennan would remain a political out-sider—until, that is, he transmitted the now famous "Long Telegram" of February 22, 1946. With Harriman away, Kennan was in charge of the embassy when there arrived from the Trea-sury Department a telegram requesting help in understanding the Soviet Union's refusal to cooperate with the World Bank and the International Monetary Fund. In reply, Kennan drafted a telegram of some eight thousand words, "all neatly divided, like an eighteenth-century Protestant sermon, into five separate parts."[68]

Rarely had a department asked for his opinion—he did not intend to allow such an opportunity to pass unseized. "They had asked for it [i.e., his opinion]," he wrote in his memoirs. "Now, by God, they would have it."[69] Because he was compos-ing a telegram, Kennan could not concern himself overmuch with style; nevertheless, he made his views crystal clear. In part one, "Basic features of postwar Soviet outlook, as put forward by official propaganda machine," he wrote that Soviet leaders believed that they were surrounded by a hostile capitalist world, with which permanent peaceful coexistence was impossible.

Because the capitalist world was beset by internal conflicts, its leaders were likely, in the Soviet view, to seek peace at home by turning aggression outward, toward the socialist world and its leader, the USSR. Such an eventuality had to be forestalled so as not to interrupt the building of socialism. To that end, everything had to be done to shore up communist parties and other "progressive" forces operating within the capitalist world. What this meant, though Kennan did not use the term, was that the Soviet Union and its allies had to wage unremitting cold war against the Western, capitalist states.

In part two, "Background of outlook," Kennan argued that the Kremlin's paranoid view of the world was rooted in Russia's traditional sense of insecurity, made worse by Marxism's in-sistence upon the inevitability and necessity of conflict. Here

Kennan touched upon an important question: namely, whether Soviet policy was based upon Marxist dogma or was better understood as a continuation of traditional Russian policy. His answer was that tradition and ideology went hand in hand—a significant modification of his earlier, almost exclusive, emphasis upon the former. The Soviet leaders did pursue expansionist goals similar to those of the tsars, but Marxism *was* important, even if Stalin was less of a true believer than Lenin. The ideology alone legitimized the regime and provided it with a program of action.

Kennan titled part three of his telegram "Projection of Soviet outlook in practical policy on official level." The Soviets, he maintained, conducted policy on two planes: official and subterranean. On the official plane they would attempt to increase the strength and prestige of the Russian state. They would participate in international organizations such as the United Nations only insofar as they served Soviet interests. In colonial or economically backward areas they would do everything within their power to weaken Western authority and influence and strengthen their own.

Kennan's artless title—it was a telegram—for part four was "Following may be said as to what we may expect by way of implementation of basic Soviet policies on unofficial, or subterranean, plane; i.e., on plane for which Soviet government accepts no responsibility." His assessment here was particularly remarkable for its accuracy and understanding. Paragraph A deserves to be quoted in full.

> Inner central core of Communist parties in other countries. While many of the persons who compose this category may also appear and act in unrelated public capacities, they are in reality working closely together as an underground operating directorate of world communism, a concealed Comintern tightly coordinated and directed by

Moscow. It is important to remember that this inner core
is actually working on underground lines, despite legality
of parties with which it is associated.[70]

As we now know, this was an almost perfect description of
what historians Harvey Klehr, John Earl Haynes, and Fridrikh
Igorevich Firsov have called the secret world of American communism. "Revisionist" historians had maintained that American communists were simply radical democrats whose only
sin was dissent from prevailing social and political norms. But
thanks to documents they collected in Russia, Klehr and his
colleagues could state with confidence that "the belief that the
American Communist movement assisted Soviet intelligence
and placed loyalty to the Soviet Union ahead of loyalty to the
United States was well founded."[71]

Kennan was also right when he observed that those communists who were involved in conspiracy and espionage constituted a minority within the party; those who made up the rank
and file were "thrust forward as bona fide internal partisans
of certain political tendencies within their respective countries,
genuinely innocent of conspiratorial connection with foreign
states."[72] According to Klehr and his colleagues, the overwhelming majority of those who passed through the American
Communist Party between 1919 and 1960 had nothing to do
with espionage.[73]

Kennan titled the fifth and final section of his telegram "Practical deductions from standpoint of US policy." It was here that
he articulated his now famous theory of "containment." Despite
its challenges, he believed that relations with the USSR could
be maintained, but only if realism governed policy. Stalin and
other Soviet leaders were opportunists who would not assume
unnecessary risks. They would withdraw when met with strong
resistance, by which Kennan did not mean—and this was
important—general military conflict. Rational, unemotional

firmness would do the trick. Deal with the Russians on a realistic and matter-of-fact basis and they would show restraint and respect, though not friendship. The effect produced in Washington by Kennan's telegram was, as he later observed, nothing less than sensational. Suddenly, he wrote in his memoirs, "my official loneliness came in fact to an end—at least for a period of two to three years. My reputation was made. My voice now carried."[74]

◆◆◆

Two months after he sent the Long Telegram, Kennan received appointment as Deputy Commandant for Foreign Affairs at the newly established National War College in Washington, D.C. He was to be responsible for the political side of the military-political curriculum. To some extent, he had Navy Secretary James Forrestal to thank for the assignment; of that tortured Princeton man, Kennan later wrote that he "was not so much himself a man of reflective and refined intelligence as he was a man who appreciated those qualities on the part of others and was anxious to see them used."[75] In any event, Kennan was most pleased, in part because his time in Bad Nauheim had given him a desire to teach, in part because he would have time to write. During his time at the college, he later recalled, his secretary typed an "endless torrent of prose."[76]

In 1991, the National Defense University Press published the lectures that Kennan delivered at the college in 1946 and 1947. In their introduction to the volume, editors Giles Harlow and George Maerz called attention not only to what Kennan had to say but to how well he said it. His literary style, they wrote, was what "one might call 'old-fashioned'—but in a grand and eloquent manner. . . . [His] prose reflects his thinking, for it is always logical, well organized, parallel, and most of all, crafted."[77]

The editors chose as their title *Measures Short of War* because in all of his lectures Kennan emphasized the importance of political—as opposed to military—means when confronting the threat posed by the Soviet Union. In the unlikely and unhappy event that the United States should find it necessary to engage the Soviets militarily, it should, in Kennan's view, think strictly in terms of limited war; he drew upon the Russian past to explain why. In modern times, he reminded students, Russia had been involved in five wars. There was, to begin with, the 1812 war with France, one of the first attempts at what might be called total war, an attempt to invade and occupy most of the territory of a foreign state. Not only did Bonaparte fail to achieve his objectives, but he drove the Russian people into the arms of their government.

The Crimean War, on the other hand, was, according to Kennan, an example of limited warfare of an eighteenth-century kind, and the results were the Russian people's disenchantment with their government, the liberation of the serfs, and the beginning of the end of tsarist rule. Another limited war, against the Japanese, hastened that end; in the midst of conflict, revolution broke out. The tsar weathered that storm, but World War I brought a fatal uprising. That war, too, in Kennan's judgment, was, while far more extensive, still limited in its aims—at least that was his view at the time. World War II, however, was unquestionably total, and because of Nazi brutality the Russians rallied around Stalin; they said to themselves, "our own people are S.O.B.'s but they are our own S.O.B.'s, and if we have to choose we will take our own."[78] The conclusion was inescapable: limited wars against Russia damaged the regime in power more than did total wars.

Concerning the Soviet regime, Kennan told his students, they should have no illusions. It was a political entity animated primarily by the desire to assure the security of its own internal political power. Soviet leaders could not be induced, by appeals to lofty ideals, to act against what they judged to be their interests. Nor were they anything but contemptuous of Western liberals who oozed admiration for the "Soviet experiment." The Kremlin leaders preferred honest and straightforward opponents who were prepared to deal with them in a businesslike, no-nonsense manner.

Unfortunately, according to Kennan, the U.S. rarely approached them in that way. In fact, the makers of American foreign policy showed no businesslike consistency of any kind. After the Bolsheviks seized power, America refused to recognize their government because they viewed diplomatic recognition as a sign of moral approval. But recognition and the establishment of formal relations should never, Kennan argued, carry with it any suggestion of moral approval or disapproval; it was always and only a matter of recognizing reality and serving the national interest. No doubt Kennan shocked some of his students when he told them that "we would deal with the devil himself if he held enough of the earth's surface to make it worthwhile for us to do so."[79] For a time, especially during the Second World War, Americans, including President Roosevelt, entertained exaggerated hopes with respect to postwar Soviet conduct and Great Power cooperation. When disillusionment set in, they became reluctant to have any dealings with the USSR.

A mature, consistent, and successful foreign policy depended upon a sense of realism and a clear-sighted defense of the national interest, but it also depended upon national strength— military, yes, but also political, economic, and moral. "Above all," Kennan insisted, national strength "is a question of our internal strength; of the health and sanity of our own society."[80] It was in *domestic affairs,* in American life, that Kennan's profound moral sensibility found expression; it was at home, he believed, that moral principles were relevant, indeed decisive. America could not, and should not, attempt to tell other people how they should live their lives—Americans' moral responsibility was for their own lives. The only way they could influence others was by example, not by preaching or coercion.

As Kennan prepared his class lectures and began to familiarize himself with the literature on war and strategy, he came to the conclusion that the existence of atomic weapons rendered total war suicidal, destructive to a degree incompatible with reason and humanity. The very concept of "total war" belonged, he knew, to the nineteenth and twentieth centuries. A return to eighteenth-century concepts of limited warfare was therefore needed. This judgment only strengthened Kennan's conviction that the nineteenth and twentieth centuries had witnessed a decline from the civilizational standards of the eighteenth. One of the virtues of the latter—and here he cited Gibbon—was "the fact that the armies of the European powers were 'exercised in [sic; the word was actually "by"] temperate and indecisive conflicts [sic; the word was "contests"].'"[81]

In an atomic age especially, Kennan was convinced, the United States had to pursue a policy of moderation. Here, too, Gibbon had said it best: "In the prosecution of a favourite scheme, the best of men, satisfied with the rectitude of their intentions, are subject to forget the bounds of moderation."[82] No wonder, then, that Kennan was drawn to Gibbon, who was, in addition to being a great historian, a literary artist of the first rank. His leisurely, flowing prose exerted a lasting influence on Kennan's own style.

One can see the influence of Gibbon's insights and artistry in the brilliant article that Kennan published in 1947. At the request of Secretary Forrestal, he had prepared a paper on Soviet conduct and the ways in which the United States might respond to it. When, after he delivered a lecture on the same subject to the Council on Foreign Relations, Hamilton Fish Armstrong asked Kennan to submit a formal statement of his views to *Foreign Affairs,* he offered, with Forrestal's permission, that which he had only recently committed to paper.

Because he was not speaking in an official capacity, Kennan signed the article with an "X." Anonymity did not long survive, but the "X article," a literary version of the Long Telegram, has remained one of the most important and controversial writings in modern American history. Kennan began by arguing that the Soviet leaders' conduct was prompted by two, mutually reinforcing influences: Marxism and Russian tradition. Each persuaded them that they were confronted by external enemies with whom no ultimate compromise was possible. To make matters worse, the existence of an external threat served as the principal justification for the continued exercise of dictatorial power.

Soviet leaders had, therefore, no choice but to adopt an aggressive stance when dealing with the outside world. And that stance produced a predictable reaction. According to Kennan, "they were soon forced, to use [a] Gibbonesque phrase, 'to chastise the contumacy' which they themselves had provoked. It is an undeniable privilege of every man to prove himself right in the thesis that the world is his enemy; for if he reiterates it frequently enough and makes it the background of his conduct he is bound eventually to be right."[83]

The Soviet leaders, then, were Marxists, but their ideology had become inextricably intertwined with their determination to retain absolute power. It was an existential phenomenon, according to Kennan, that Gibbon had described better than anyone else. "From enthusiasm to imposture," the Englishman had written, "the step is perilous and slippery; the demon of Socrates affords a memorable instance of how a wise man may deceive himself, how a good man may deceive others, how the conscience may slumber in a mixed and middle state between self-illusion and voluntary fraud."[84]

Dealing with such men presented a challenge, but Kennan pointed out that their faith in the inevitable victory over "capitalism" meant that they were in no great hurry. Like Russian leaders before them, they took the long view and were prepared to be patient; they would advance where they could and continue to apply pressure everywhere, but when confronted by determined resistance they were prepared to retreat.

It was important to bear in mind, Kennan wrote, that while the Soviet leaders were neither reckless nor impatient, they were persistent. They could not be countered by episodic actions inspired by "the momentary whims of democratic opinion," but only by the "long-term, patient but firm and vigilant containment of Russian expansive tendencies."[85] Although to his subsequent regret he did not make it clear, Kennan had in mind political, rather than military, confrontation and containment. The Soviet leaders' caution and historical confidence militated against a military gamble, particularly in the face of nuclear weapons. Any resort to violence would almost certainly be domestic in character.

The political containment of Soviet power would, Kennan knew, require patience and steadiness of nerve, but it was likely to pay handsome dividends. Almost alone among Kremlin watchers—Andrei Amalrik and Bernard Levin came much later—Kennan believed that, in time, the internal contradictions of Soviet rule would lead to the disintegration and ultimate disappearance of the USSR. While Soviet leaders could boast of some achievements in heavy industry, for example, their overall handling of the economy left much to be desired. And, unlike Soviet admirers in the West, most Russians were disillusioned with both the theory and practice of Marxism.

Kennan also suggested that Stalin's death, when it came, could lead to a crisis of leadership. In fact it did, though the Soviet Union managed to survive. But when Mikhail Gorbachev came to power, the kind of disunity at the top that Kennan had thought possible did mean that, as he put it in his X article, "the chaos and weakness of Russian society would be revealed in forms beyond description." His conclusion concerning the survivability of the Soviet Union was prescient: "[T]he possibility remains (and in the opinion of this writer it is a strong one) that Soviet power, like the capitalist world of its conception, bears within it the seeds of its own decay, and that the sprouting of these seeds is well advanced."[86]

In the final section of the X article, Kennan argued that the containment which he recommended would have a greater chance of success if the United States set for the world, including the communist world, an example of self-confidence, maturity, and rectitude. It could ill afford the kind of internal decay of which, in later years, he was to take a highly critical and profoundly pessimistic view.

By the time the X article appeared, Kennan had left the War College to become director of the State Department's new Policy Planning Staff. Secretary George C. Marshall wanted to draw upon expert and deliberative judgment when identifying America's long-term foreign policy objectives; it was the kind of professional approach that appealed to Kennan. "The essence of planning," he had told his War College students, "is keeping yourself free of trivialities and concentrating on pure thought."[87] Because of the pressure of Cold War events, however, he and the members of his small staff soon found that they had primarily to concern themselves with existing problems and crises, admittedly not trivial in nature; although that bothered Kennan, it made it possible for him to influence foreign policy to a greater degree than he ever had before or ever would again.

Kennan set about his new work with enthusiasm and very definite principles. He believed that the threat posed by the Soviet Union, though real, was political rather than military in character. It was therefore imperative that areas vital to America's national interest and vulnerable to communist subversion be politically stable and economically strong. While seeking to frustrate communist efforts, however, he rejected the notion that those with responsibility for foreign policy should base their decisions upon some "doctrine" that possessed universal applicability. It was precisely for that reason that he had objected to the so-called "Truman Doctrine," announced by President Truman before a joint session of Congress on March 12, 1947.

While still at the War College, he had been summoned by Under Secretary of State Dean Acheson to participate in deliberations concerning the British government's decision to end its special aid to Greece, which was then facing a communist insurgency. On being apprised of the situation, Kennan opined that the U.S. should not consider sending troops, because it was not "clear as to when and how we would get them out."[88] He did think, however, that economic aid should be extended to the Greeks. While the establishment of a communist dictatorship in the homeland of Western civilization might not be disastrous from the standpoint of U.S. interests, it could well have unfortunate and long-term strategic consequences.

For Kennan, providing aid to Greece would represent an attempt to solve a particular problem. When, therefore, he was shown a draft of the speech the president planned to deliver, he was dismayed and disturbed. At the center of that now historic speech were these oft-quoted words: "I believe that it must be the policy of the United States to support free peoples who are resisting attempted subjugation by armed minorities or by outside pressures. I believe that we must assist free peoples to work out their own destinies in their own way." A policy that aimed to address a quite specific set of circumstances had become a "doctrine" possessing universal validity. Not only Greece, but Turkey as well was to receive aid, and the door was left open for any country that could demonstrate the existence of a communist threat to claim American help—and this without any consideration of the particular exigencies of the situation.

"We like," Kennan wrote in the chapter of his memoirs devoted to the Truman Doctrine, "to attribute a universal significance to decisions we have already found it necessary, for limited and parochial reasons, to take. It was not enough for us, when circumstances forced us into World War I, to hold in view the specific reasons for our entry: our war effort had to be clothed in the form of an effort to make the *world* (nothing less) 'safe for democracy.'"[89] Each region of the world, indeed each country, had, in his view, to be dealt with on an individual basis. He believed also that the U.S. would have to recognize its limitations; it could not act anywhere and everywhere in the world.

Unfortunately, because of what Kennan later called "the careless and indiscriminate language of the X-article," Walter Lippmann, whom he knew well and greatly respected, concluded that as the theorist of containment he was the architect of the Truman Doctrine. In *The Cold War: A Study in U.S. Foreign Policy* (1947), the renowned columnist pointed out that that doctrine "must in practice mean inexorably an unending intervention in all the countries that are supposed to 'contain' the Soviet Union,"[90] and he set the Marshall Plan over against it. Kennan was mortified by Lippmann's misunderstanding but concluded that he had no one to blame but himself.

Far from opposing the Marshall Plan, Kennan strongly supported it. In fact, in his judicious study of the Policy Planning Staff (PPS) years, Wilson Miscamble pointed out that Kennan played a crucial role in the plan's early development. On May 23, 1947, he forwarded to Under Secretary of State Acheson the recently established (May 5) Policy Planning Staff's first recommendation—to provide economic aid to Western Europe. The staff, Kennan wrote, considered that such aid "should be directed not to the combating of communism as such but to the restoration of the economic health and vigor of European society. It should aim, in other words, to combat not communism, but the economic maladjustment which makes European society vulnerable to exploitation by any and all totalitarian movements and which Russian communism is now exploiting."[91] It emphasized that Europeans should take primary responsibility for drafting a recovery program, with Americans playing a secondary role.

In the same recommendation, Kennan added a section calling for a public clarification of the Truman Doctrine. It must be made clear, he wrote, that the doctrine did not constitute a "blank check to give economic and military aid to any area in the world where the communists show signs of being successful."[92] Aid to Greece and Turkey was to be regarded as a particular remedy for a particular problem.

Two weeks later, on June 5, 1947, Secretary of State Marshall delivered his famous "Marshall Plan" speech at Harvard; it reflected total acceptance of the PPS recommendation. "Our policy," the secretary told the university's graduating class, "is directed not against any country or doctrine but against hunger, poverty, desperation, and chaos." And he made it clear that his government had no intention of drawing up "unilaterally a program designed to place Europe on its feet economically. This is the business of Europeans. The initiative, I think, must come from Europe. The role of this country should consist of friendly aid in the drafting of a European program and of later support of such a program so far as it may be practical for us to do so."[93]

We now know that for Kennan the Marshall Plan was an overt act of political warfare. Over the course of the next year, he convinced himself that covert actions would also be necessary in order to meet the Soviet challenge. In a Policy Planning Staff memorandum dated May 4, 1948, he warned that "having been engaged by the full might of the Kremlin's political warfare, we cannot afford to leave unmobilized our resources for covert political warfare." Covert actions might include "liberation committees" of political refugees from the Soviet world and the support of indigenous anticommunist elements in threatened countries of the Free World.[94]

On June 18, the National Security Council endorsed the proposal as NSC 10/2, which established the Office of Special Projects, soon renamed the Office of Policy Coordination (OPC), in the CIA; Frank Wisner, a Kennan friend, was entrusted with the directorship. Kennan was later to call his pivotal role in promoting the plan "the greatest mistake I ever made,"[95] and in a piece for the *New York Times* that he wrote late in life he stated his conviction, based upon his long experience as a government official and as a historian, that the need for secret intelligence about affairs elsewhere in the world had been vastly overrated. Because most information could be found by careful study of legitimate sources, the often lurid games played by spies and counterspies could, without damage to national security, be ended. Methods of deception, he warned, exact a price, "for they inculcate in their authors, as well as their intended victims, unlimited cynicism, causing them to lose all realistic understanding of the interrelationship, in what they are doing, of ends and means."[96]

He did not say anything to readers of the *Times* about his own role in authorizing covert actions—as he had in his memoirs—but he did point out that in Stalin's time "the almost psychotic preoccupation of the Communist regime with secrecy appeared to many, not unnaturally, to place a special premium on efforts to penetrate that curtain by secretive methods of our own."[97] Out of a similar conviction, he had also approved of and associated himself with the cultural cold war waged by the Congress for Cultural Freedom, organized during the summer of 1950 in conjunction with a West Berlin conference of anticommunist intellectuals.

The idea for the conference had originated with Melvin J. Lasky, then employed by the U.S. military government in Berlin to edit the sophisticated anticommunist journal *Der Monat;* Sidney Hook, the American philosopher and social critic; Ruth Fischer (Eisler), a tough and intelligent ex-communist; and

Franz Borkenau, a onetime functionary of the Communist International. Officially, *Der Monat* would sponsor the congress, while unofficially—in fact, secretly—the CIA would provide the needed money.

The congress attracted an impressive group of intellectuals, including Arthur Koestler, Michael Polanyi, the distinguished physical chemist turned philosopher, and Raymond Aron, who engaged pro-Soviet intellectuals such as Jean-Paul Sartre and Maurice Merleau-Ponty in debate—to their considerable disadvantage. Members of the congress displayed an almost studied incuriosity about the source of its money, in part because they believed World War III to be at hand, and in part because they were not asked to do anything they did not sincerely wish to do.

Kennan made that point when, after the funding source became public knowledge, the congress came under heavy attack. "The flap about C.I.A. money," he told the Ford Foundation's Shepard Stone, "was quite unwarranted, and caused far more anguish than it should have been permitted to cause. I never felt the slightest pangs of conscience about it. . . . This country has no ministry of culture, and C.I.A. was obliged to do what it could to try to fill the gap. It should be praised for having done so, and not criticized."[98]

Most congress members were left-leaning liberals or democratic socialists, but there were some who did not answer to either description—Polanyi, Aron, Bertrand de Jouvenel, and Eric Voegelin, for example. Kennan represented the most conservative point of view. In his closing address to the congress's Milan conference ("The Future of Freedom"), held September 12–17, 1955, he startled the socialists by saying that "all that equalizes, all that levels, all that standardizes is the enemy of freedom."[99] And in a paper delivered in Basel at a conference on "Industrial Society and Western Political Dialogue" (September 20–26, 1959), he made it clear that his call for a high degree of *dirigisme* did not mean that he had embraced socialism, even in its moderate form.

Indeed it did not. *Dirigisme* means governmental direction and control of the economy, but not in the socialist sense. It refers to an economy based upon private ownership of the means of production, but subject to government regulation. Kennan had primarily in mind the setting of limits to the workings of the free market, particularly with respect to large enterprises and to the uses to which nature may be put. He was not, then, seeking to remedy "social injustice," but to rectify the injustice that mankind was doing to itself by permitting the machine to become its master rather than its servant, by adopting a rapacious and irresponsible attitude toward nature, and by sinking into the morass of passive recreation, commercialized aesthetic media, and a dreary egalitarianism of the spirit.[100]

Lasky and his colleagues had not chosen West Berlin as the venue for the congress's founding conference at random. Like most people who gave the matter more than a passing thought, they believed that Germany held the key to Europe's future. It is safe to say, however, that few others felt the kind of sympathy for the country that Kennan did. His father, who admired German culture, had taken him, as a boy, to Kassel for six months; as an adult, he had lived in Germany for a total of more than five years and spoke the language fluently.

In his memoirs, it is true, Kennan wrote that "it was a country with which I was never able to identify extensively in the personal sense," but in the same paragraph, he confessed that "intellectually and aesthetically, Germany had made a deep impression on me."[101] In part, that was a result of his great admiration for Helmuth von Moltke and other members of the

German opposition to Hitler. But he also respected Bismarck and the pre–World War I German political tradition. At war's end, for example, he had drafted a memo in which he argued that "the only reasonably respectable tradition of orderly and humane government in Germany is actually that of a strong monarchical government."[102] His view of the matter was of course ignored.

In order to gain a clearer picture of life in postwar Germany, Kennan had visited Berlin, Frankfurt, and Hamburg in March 1949. What he saw in the third city, where he had held his first permanent foreign service post, sickened him. From July 24 to August 3, 1943, the Allies—primarily the Royal Air Force— had subjected that unfortunate city to a series of devastating air raids, code-named Operation Gomorrah. On one night (July 27–28) nearly eight hundred bombers unloaded thousands of tons of high explosives and incendiary bombs that created an unimaginable firestorm. One German fire warden recalled the inferno this way: "Then a storm started, a shrill howling in the street. It grew into a hurricane. . . . The whole yard, the canal, in fact as far as we could see, was just a whole, great, massive sea of fire."[103] Thirty-five thousand men, women, and children perished as a result of the attack. Allied historians later called it "The Battle of Hamburg"; Germans called it *"die Katastrophe."* Six years later, Kennan discovered sweeping devastation, mile after mile.

"And here, for the first time," he wrote in his diaries, "I felt an unshakable conviction that no momentary military advantage . . . could have justified this stupendous, careless destruction of civilian life and of material values, built up laboriously by human hands over the course of centuries for purposes having nothing to do with this war."[104] Area, or carpet, bombing of that kind exceeded moral limits; such a conscious policy of destruction, Paul Johnson has written, "marked a critical stage in the moral declension of humanity in our times."[105]

The British philosopher A. C. Grayling has made the same argument in a carefully reasoned study of the bombing of civilians and the near obliteration of cultures in Germany and Japan. "If," he wrote, "the war in either the European or the Pacific theatre had lasted months more, or another year, with the area-bombing campaigns continuing their intensifying curve, the impression given would be one of an attempt at annihilation."[106] Such an attempt could not satisfy the criteria for a just military action as distilled from the collective moral wisdom of mankind—namely, that such an action must be both necessary and proportionate to winning the war.

Kennan would certainly have agreed. He deplored what he called the military mind's obsession "with the concept of destruction—sheer destruction, destruction for its own sake—as the central aim of warfare."[107] The true aim of war, in his view, was not to annihilate the enemy but to change his frame of mind to one more consistent with peaceful behavior. He recognized that in the aftermath of the war, few in the West agreed with him—hatred for, and fear of, Germany ran too deep. He therefore argued for German unification and the embedding of a united Germany in a united Western Europe.

Kennan knew, of course, that Eastern Europe was not free to join the West, but unlike most observers, he remained convinced that its captivity was not permanent. In a Policy Planning Staff Paper of November 6, 1947, he wrote that it was "unlikely that approximately one hundred million Russians will succeed in holding down permanently, in addition to their own minorities, some ninety millions of Europeans with a higher cultural level and with long experience in resistance to foreign rule."[108]

We now know that he was right. But his insight tells us something also about his realism. Although he certainly sympathized with the Eastern Europeans, he knew that there was little that the U.S. could do about their contemporary predicament. True, after Stalin read Yugoslavia out of the Cominform in 1948, he saw a chance of improved relations with Marshal Tito, but he counseled a cautious approach.

Kennan's views may have seemed to some to be too passive in the face of communist aggression or too indifferent to the fates of large numbers of human beings. James Burnham, for one, thought "containment" too defensive and argued for the "liberation" of those under communist rule.[109] Writing in 1952, the former Trotskyite spoke of preparing for general war, though he did not, he said, think it likely. Kennan seems never to have read Burnham's book, probably because he thought talk of liberation was for those who hoped for World War III but were unwilling to say so.

In retrospect, Kennan's was the wiser and more responsible policy. For him, as for Richelieu and Bismarck, sympathy for foreigners, or considerations of justice and morality, could not be permitted to affect judgment concerning the national interest. That is why he opposed American support for the creation of Israel. That support, he recognized, would entail serious responsibilities. "I see no reason," he wrote to a friend in 1956, eight years after the creation of the new state, "why we should work ourselves into positions which tend to make the State of Israel a permanent ward and military liability of the United States." He then added a realistic assessment of the possibility of peace in the Middle Eastern region. "It has been perfectly clear from the beginning that a Jewish state could be maintained in that area only by force of arms; there was no justification whatsoever for any other hope."[110]

Kennan was equally opposed to efforts to maintain Chiang Kai-shek in power in China. The generalissimo could not be saved without an American intervention and such an intervention would be ill-advised, particularly in view of the fact that of the Far Eastern countries, Japan was, in his judgment, far more important to U.S. interests. Of the Chinese in general, he had long ago formed a negative opinion.

Kennan won some of his battles, but he lost others—his government supported the creation of Israel and of NATO, which he also opposed because it reflected too great a preoccupation with military rivalry and was likely to congeal the division of Europe. As time wore on, he became ever more convinced that few persons in positions of power shared or even understood his political realism, or what in one particular context he referred to as "a cool and unemotional appraisal of national interest."[111] He decided to step down as director of the Policy Planning Staff and, in June 1950, to take a long leave of absence—without pay—from government service. It would give him the leisure and the freedom to formulate his approach to the great questions facing his country without the restraints imposed upon him as a government employee.

Before he could depart, however, North Korea invaded the South. On hearing the news he knew that the incursion would have to be met with resistance—a response to a provocation—but he argued that military action should have the limited goal of advancing only to the former demarcation line along the Thirty-Eighth Parallel. To advance beyond that point, even if militarily feasible, would be to risk a far broader war that might eventually involve the Russians or the Chinese. As we know, the government, or rather General MacArthur, refused to heed Kennan's warning, with what result—the massive intervention of the Chinese—we also know.

America's dangerous, and failed, effort to overrun North Korea increased Kennan's feelings of despair concerning the future of civilization. So did the official trip to Latin America that he had taken the preceding February. In the trip report he prepared for the secretary of state, he dwelt upon what seemed to him to be the tragic nature of human civilization in the countries south of the United States. Geography, climate, and history all seemed to conspire against them—in ways that they did not in North America. It was therefore difficult to know what institutions of government were morally commendable in any Latin American country.

Of one thing, however, Kennan was certain: it could not be assumed that America's institutions would answer to the requirements of other lands. They grew out of a particular experience of a particular people, and "any attempt on our part to recommend [them] to others must come perilously close to the messianic tendencies of those militant political ideologies which say, in effect, 'You should believe because we believe.'"[112]

So shocked was the assistant secretary for Latin America by Kennan's report that he persuaded Acheson to forbid its distribution within the State Department and to lock all copies away. Had he known of them, he would probably have confiscated Kennan's private diaries as well. On the train from Washington to Mexico City, the counselor of the department reflected upon the menace that cities posed to civilization. "For cities," he mused as the train sped by an industrial area, "there is something sinister and pitiless about the dawn. . . . In [its] chill, calm light, the city is helpless, and in a sense, naked. Its dreams are disturbed, its pretense, its ugliness, its impermanence exposed, its failure documented, its verdict written, the darkness, with its neon signs, its eroticism, and its intoxication, was protective and forgiving—tolerant of dreams and of delusions. The dawn is judgment: merciless and impassive."[113]

It is difficult to imagine another American diplomat thinking such thoughts or expressing them in such language. His diary entries reveal the other—the real—George Kennan, a man who, in his most intimate life, was anything but "cool and unemotional." His public persona—the cool, detached realist—satisfied two demands: to subordinate his own interests to those of the country he served and to shield him from any uninvited intrusion into his private world. Those identities would continue to coexist as he moved to Princeton, where J. Robert Oppenheimer had offered him the hospitality of the Institute for Advanced Study. Kennan would forever be grateful to Oppenheimer for the confidence the director placed in his future as a scholar, a confidence that was not initially shared by all of the institute's permanent members.

◆◆◆

Founded by educator Abraham Flexner with money provided by Newark philanthropist Louis Bamberger and his sister, Mrs. Felix Fuld, the Institute for Advanced Study identifies itself as "an independent, private institution devoted to the encouragement, support and patronage of learning. . . . [It was] founded in 1930 as a community of scholars where intellectual inquiry could be carried out in the most favorable circumstances."[114] The circumstances were—and are—most favorable indeed. Members of the institute, permanent and visiting, devote themselves to their research and writing without having to shoulder any other responsibility.

They do not have to conduct classes or attend seminars or deliver lectures. They have comfortable offices and access to institute and Princeton University libraries. They work "protected against the noise and bustle of urban or commercial life,"[115] surrounded by the natural beauty of an eight-hundred-acre site that boasts the magnificent and tranquil Institute Woods. No one who has walked the woods' trails will ever forget them. Kennan certainly never did. "I have lived in the proximity of these Woods for over half a century," he once said. "They are a friend, a source of inspiration and restoration, and were they to disappear it would be like the disappearance of an old, beloved, and respected friend."[116]

For Kennan, as for many others, the institute was a foretaste of the heaven reserved for scholars; "quiet, ascetic, devoid of distracting activities" was the way he described it in his memoirs.[117] Among those who called it home were Albert Einstein and John von Neumann, formulator of game theory and pioneer of computer science. Both men were original members of the institute's first school, the School of Mathematics (it then included physicists as well as mathematicians). Out of respect for his privacy, and because he understood little or nothing of the great physicist's work, Kennan never met Einstein. But of course he knew and admired Oppenheimer and was awed by the learning upon which art historian Erwin Panofsky and medievalist Ernst Kantorowicz could draw.

In a community of such intelligence, Kennan felt, and began to dwell upon, what he took to be his personal inadequacies. "The private diaries," he wrote in his memoirs, "now began to contain more in the way of self-reproaches, complaints of the vanity of current preoccupations, protests about the aimlessness of one's existence, yearnings for a greater unity and seriousness of purpose."[118] It was not merely his inability to place American foreign policy on a more secure footing. At the core of his discontent was his awareness that his active engagement with daily and pressing governmental affairs had prevented him from doing the kind of writing that he believed he was born to do—work that possessed literary value and that reflected his true self. He was determined to dedicate the time remaining to him to the composition of works of more than fleeting significance.

He was, however, restless; it was difficult to adjust to a quiet life. So he accepted invitations to deliver lectures, including entire lecture series. While he was still in government service, the University of Chicago had invited him to deliver the series sponsored by the Charles B. Walgreen Foundation. In April 1951, he traveled to the Windy City by train—his preferred means of land transportation. He took a taxi to the South Side, checked into his hotel, and went for his customary walk. He did not much like what he observed on the city streets—dirt, unkempt people, aimless youths, lonely old men. When he returned to the hotel he wrote in his diary: "You have despaired of yourself; now despair of your country!"[119]

It was in such a mood that Kennan delivered a series of brilliant and superbly crafted lectures under the collective title "American Diplomacy 1900–1950." Taken together, the lectures constituted a carefully reasoned critique of America's legalistic-moralistic approach to the conduct of foreign policy—"the belief that it should be possible to suppress the chaotic and dangerous aspirations of governments in the international field by the acceptance of some system of legal rules and restraints."[120] That belief entailed the transferring into the affairs of states ideas of individual right and wrong, the subjecting of state behavior to moral judgment.

To substitute moral judgment for the adjustment of competing national interests—the meaning of diplomacy—made it far more difficult, should states enter a military contest, to stop short of total victory; and a goal of total victory could only mean a willingness, if necessary, to fight a total war. "It is a curious thing," Kennan told his audience, "that the legalistic approach to world affairs, rooted as it unquestionably is in a desire to do away with war and violence, makes violence more enduring, more terrible, and more destructive to political stability than did the older motives of national interest."[121] By turning the Great War into a moral crusade, for example, Woodrow Wilson made it difficult, if not impossible, to settle for anything less than total victory, with the result that the European balance of power, which had maintained the peace with few and limited exceptions for a century, was upset and a resentful Germany was made ready for Hitler.

There was nothing wrong intrinsically, Kennan argued, with the pursuance of national interest or the recognition of power realities. The United States should take the latter "as existing and inalterable human forces, neither good nor bad, and . . .

seek their point of maximum equilibrium rather than their re-form or their repression."[122] Such an approach would reduce the chances of war and, should it come, limit its extent with respect to both ends and means.

Kennan was less than optimistic that the approach he rec-ommended would be adopted by the United States, because it did not fit comfortably into a democratic system. There was, to begin with, the problem of public opinion: so easily excit-ed by demagogues, so ready to view international problems through a moral prism, so ignorant of the world beyond Amer-ica's shores—but so able to bring pressure to bear upon those charged with responsibility for the conduct of foreign policy. And those so charged were themselves not invariably well pre-pared for duty. Too often they were dilettantes, friends of the president. Without holding out much hope, Kennan argued for a greater degree of professionalism in the diplomatic service.

This pessimism concerning the conduct of American foreign policy was of a piece with Kennan's pessimism with respect to America. A trip to southern California on behalf of the Ford Foundation did nothing to reduce his mounting fears for the future of his country. Appalled by Californians' dependence upon the automobile, preoccupation with physical beauty and prowess, and eagerness to escape responsibility, he wrote in his diary that the Los Angeles area "is childhood without the prom-ise of maturity."[123] It was the rest of America, or what the rest of America would soon be, and he shuddered at the thought.

Kennan's spirits lifted on those occasions when he was able to visit Europe. Because his wife was Norwegian, he and his family made many trips to Norway. On a journey taken in July 1951, after having delivered his Chicago lectures and before he traveled to California, he recorded some impressions in his diary that radiated peace and joy. From the deck of a Norwe-gian-American ocean liner—Kennan always preferred ships to planes—he looked down on the town of Stavanger:

Everything so compact, so neat, so sedate, yet so full of
life: warehouses, offices, stores, all doing business before
our eyes; bicyclists, horses and carts, people standing in
the sunshine just looking at the great ship above them,
piles of cargo piled up on the street at shipside. This was a
harbor street as harbor streets were meant to be, teeming
with life, with sociability, with the intimacy of ship and
shore.[124]

Stalin's Russia was, alas, not Norway, and it was in the former that Kennan was soon to take up residence for a last time.
Sometime after returning from California, he was contacted by
Secretary of State Acheson and informed that President Truman wished to appoint him to succeed the retiring Admiral
Alan Kirk as U.S. ambassador to the Soviet Union. His whole
career having prepared him for such a dignity, Kennan accepted the appointment and was quickly and easily confirmed.
After frustrating and ultimately futile efforts to obtain instruc-
tions, he set out, arriving in Moscow on May 5, 1952.

Things went badly from the beginning; the Russians received him coldly. Perhaps because he had been away from
Russia for so long or because he was now chief of the U.S. mission, he found it "impossible to adjust comfortably to the incredible volume and hatefulness of lies these people manage to
put out about us and themselves and everyone."[125] Moreover, he
chafed more than ever under the restrictions placed upon him
by the Soviet government. In a report filled with frustration, he
informed President Truman that "we are so cut off and hemmed
in with restrictions and ignored by the Soviet government that
it is as though no diplomatic relations existed at all."[126] He was
not, therefore, in a good mood when, in the middle of September, he left Moscow to attend a London conference of U.S. ambassadors serving in Europe. On the way, the plane carrying
him made a stop at Tempelhof airport in Berlin and he was be-

sieged by reporters, one of whom asked whether he had many social contacts with Russians.

Irritated by the ignorance the question betrayed, Kennan snapped back, "Don't you know how foreign diplomats live in Moscow?" When the reporter allowed that he did not know, Kennan responded undiplomatically: "I was interned here in Germany for several months during the last war. The treatment we receive in Moscow is just about like the treatment we internees received then, except that in Moscow we are at liberty to go out and walk the streets under guard."[127] "Slanderer Under the Mask of Diplomat," *Pravda* screamed. The Soviet government informed the U.S. embassy in Moscow that Kennan had been declared *persona non grata*.

Because, however, he knew the real reason for his expulsion, Kennan was not inclined to apologize. "While I am sure," he wrote to Bernard Gufler, a foreign service colleague with whom he had enjoyed many a philosophic discussion,

> that people in the Department are reproaching me for "indiscretion," I have a good conscience about the matter. I know they would not have expelled me unless I had succeeded in making them uncomfortable; and they would not have been made uncomfortable unless they had felt that I was coming too close to the exposure of some of their frauds and outrages, which it seems to me it was my job to do.[128]

Shortly after the 1952 election of General Dwight D. Eisenhower, Kennan and his family sailed for the United States. Upon reaching New York, they made their way to their Pennsylvania farm. There Kennan waited until March, when the new secretary of state, John Foster Dulles, summoned him to Washington and informed him that there was no place for him in the department or in the foreign service. Naturally enough, Kennan did not take kindly to such shabby treatment, particularly from a fellow Princetonian, a fellow Presbyterian, and a man who wore his religious faith on his sleeve. He told his friend Louis J. Halle that Dulles "did not have an ounce of real piety in his system; the hypocrisy was pure, as was the ambition. Both were unadulterated by any tinges of genuine Christian charity or obligation."[129]

In the same month that Dulles unburdened the State Department of Kennan, Charles "Chip" Bohlen was sworn in as the new U.S. ambassador to Moscow. Under the rules then governing the foreign service, if a former ambassador did not receive appointment elsewhere within three months, he would be retired automatically; thus it was that Kennan was retired, effective June 1953. As he cleaned out a desk that he had been given for temporary use, it occurred to him that, having completed twenty-seven years of service with a great organization, he should say goodbye to someone before leaving, but he could not think of anyone and was grateful to be able to take his leave of a receptionist. He was to devote the remainder of his life—with one brief interlude—to teaching and, above all, to writing.

# 2

## The Institute for Advanced Study

The Institute for Advanced Study provided Kennan with time and a near-perfect environment for the historical research and writing he so longed to undertake. And yet he did not find it easy to settle down to a monastic life. For one thing, travel was in his blood. He was happy to accept an invitation, extended in 1955, to serve as Eastman Professor at Balliol College, Oxford, for the 1957–58 academic year. He took up residence in England in August 1957, and before his wife and four children could join him, wrote in his diary of "endless loneliness—days without the exchange of a single social word. Long walks in the fresh, damp wind."[1] During those times alone he could, and probably did, think about the Reith Lectures that he had agreed to deliver on the BBC.

Bertrand Russell, Arnold Toynbee, and his Princeton colleague J. Robert Oppenheimer had delivered previous lectures and Kennan was flattered to be included in their company. He soon learned that live radio could be intimidating, but he managed nevertheless to acquit himself well. Acutely aware of the dismay and fear occasioned by the launching of Sputnik, the world's first artificial satellite, on October 4, 1957 (on the eve, that is, of his first lecture), Kennan cautioned his listeners not to make too much of Soviet achievements. The Kremlin rulers faced serious problems, not the least of which was an intelligent-sia that was beginning to ask pointed questions.

As usual, Kennan emphasized the political nature of the Soviet threat and insisted that it could be met by firm, consistent, and informed policies. He expressed skepticism concerning the value of summit meetings, coalition diplomacy, and the United Nations and urged "the patient, quiet, orderly use of the regular channels of private communication between governments, as they have grown up and proved their worth over the course of the centuries."[2] Only in that way, he argued, could anything constructive be done about the unnatural division of Europe.

Kennan regarded as unrealistic and unreasonable any idea that the U.S. and its allies could have their way in the heart of the old continent; the Soviet Union would never agree to a unified Germany that looked to membership in NATO. That did not mean, however, that nothing could be done to reduce tensions and thus reduce the risk of nuclear war. The Soviets had indicated a willingness to discuss a mutual withdrawal of military forces from Europe's center; why not put their seriousness to the test? Negotiation would have to be kept from public view and compromise would be necessary, but that was only another way of saying that the two sides would have to engage in diplomacy.

But what was most striking about Kennan's Reith Lectures was the emphasis he placed, as he always did, upon putting the U.S. and other Western nations' houses in order—upon, that is, moral renewal and the restoration of national discipline. "To my own countrymen who have often asked me where best to apply the hand to counter the Soviet threat, I have," he said, "had to reply: to our American failings—to the things we are ashamed of in our own eyes: to the racial problem, to the conditions in our big cities, to the education and environment of our young people, to the growing gap between specialized knowledge and popular understanding."[3] For Kennan, the real threat to the U.S. and Western civilization in general was internal decay, not external enemies. "In a thousand ways," in fact, "the tone and spirit that characterizes our internal life impinge themselves on our external fortunes."[4] Something, he believed, that one could also say of individual human beings.

To Kennan's surprise, his lectures touched exposed nerves. True, he received much praise. In the *Reporter,* Max Ascoli heralded "the thoughts of a lonely man who is not very much at home in his own land."[5] Michael Polanyi wrote to say that he had been "profoundly moved by the first of your Reith Lectures to which I listened last night," and to suggest that the Congress for Cultural Freedom would be happy to disseminate and discuss his ideas.[6] From the Institute for Advanced Study, Ernst Kantorowicz sent his congratulations.

In addition to praise, however, there was criticism of Kennan's opposition to the development of more powerful nuclear weapons and to any first-strike strategy; his talk of mutual withdrawal from Germany; and his coolness toward NATO. Friends such as Raymond Aron and Walter Lippmann took him to task for espousing "unrealistic" ideas. The Frenchman even argued that a clear division in Europe was less dangerous than any other arrangement. Taken aback, Kennan concluded that his was a voice crying in the wilderness and that there was little point in continuing to beat his head against the wall; after composing an extended rebuttal to his critics, he decided not to publish it. It would be wiser, he concluded, to turn to history, "the common refuge of those who find themselves helpless in the face of the present."[7]

But Kennan had no intention of withdrawing into the past. He still wished to speak to his country and the West, even if less directly. He was drawn to history because he believed that the past contained important lessons for the present. In that sense, as his friend, the historian John Lukacs, has pointed out, he did not intend to write "pure" history.[8] He did intend, however, to dispel any thought of historical inevitability; history was contingent because men possessed free will. That meant that their destiny depended upon their own decisions and actions—hence the importance of learning how they had decided and acted in the past, and with what consequences. To be sure, no situation was ever exactly the same as another, but that did not mean that there were no similarities. The study of history could thus serve as both guide and cautionary tale.

It was with thoughts such as these that Kennan delivered his Oxford lectures, subsequently published, along with some delivered at Harvard, as *Russia and the West Under Lenin and Stalin* (1961). With few exceptions, he treated Western relations with late-tsarist and Soviet Russia as a cautionary tale, beginning his story with the folly of 1914. "I should like to make my own position clear," he told his students. "I hold the First World War to have been *the* great catastrophe of Western civilization in the present century."[9] It was the war that brought down the government of the tsar, and it was Alexander Kerensky's decision to continue the war that doomed the Russian Provisional Government. What was more, much of the diplomatic success achieved by the Soviet regime was the result of the West's social and spiritual exhaustion.

And what was it all for? Imperial Germany, Kennan conceded, was a problem, but it was not *such* a problem. In fact, nothing that was at stake in the years leading up to the outbreak of hostilities was of such importance that it justified a conflict so bloody and self-defeating. As we know, Kennan regarded all modern wars as self-defeating; no conceivable gain could outweigh losses. What one might call the logic of total war made it impossible to end the fighting short of total victory, and that meant a staggering loss of life. In order to justify that loss, democracies easily convinced themselves that civilization itself required that they prevail.

As Kennan observed, however, a German victory "would not have been quite *such* a catastrophe."[10] Rather the contrary, one might suggest. Had Germany won the war there would have been no Nazi regime, no Soviet regime (the Germans would not have left Lenin in power), no Auschwitz, no Gulag Archipelago. The Germans would, for a time, have dominated Europe, but they would have been led by the Kaiser, not by Hitler. Thanks to the Western powers' insistence upon a complete military victory over Germany, the world was not spared any of the above—beginning with the Bolshevik coup d'état.

Throughout his analyses of pivotal moments in Soviet-Western relations, Kennan showed a certain respect—too great in some instances—for Lenin and other Bolsheviks. Lenin, he told his students, believed "in using violence only to the extent that it was absolutely necessary in order to promote one's political ends. He had no particular liking for it, I think."[11] That, we now know, is not true. In his important biography, the late Dmitri Volkogonov, who had access to archival material never before available, demonstrated conclusively that the Bolshevik leader lusted for blood: "The idea of the concentration camp system—the State Camp Administration, or GULAG—and the appalling purges of the 1930s are commonly associated with the name of Stalin, but the true father of the Bolshevik concentration camps, the executions, the mass terror and the 'organs' which stood above the state, was Lenin."[12]

When asked, when both were safely dead, to compare Lenin and Stalin, Vyacheslav Molotov, who had reason to know, replied that the former had been the "more severe." Recently published documents bear this out. In an August 11, 1918, directive to authorities in the province of Penza, where peasants had protested grain confiscations, Lenin ordered that they be "mercilessly suppressed. . . . Hang (hang without fail, so the people see) no fewer than one hundred known kulaks, rich men, bloodsuckers. . . . Take from them all the grain." On March 19, 1922, he sent a top secret memorandum to members of the Politburo concerning the Russian Orthodox Church's efforts to prevent the looting of churches. We must, he wrote, battle the clergy "in the most decisive and merciless manner and crush its resistance with such brutality that it will not forget it for decades to come." As the writer Maxim Gorky once wrote, Lenin's love for mankind "looked far ahead, through the mists of hatred."[13]

Concerning Stalin, Kennan was less deceived; he had, after all, witnessed the purges and the Great Terror. Nevertheless, while perfectly well aware of the Man of Steel's ruthlessness and cunning, he described him in his memoirs as one of the great men of the age. And so, he insisted, was Hitler. "Hitler was a dangerous man: fanatical, brutal, unreliable, capable of the most breath-taking duplicity. But he was by no means a mountebank; and if it be conceded that evil can be great, then the quality of greatness cannot, I think, be denied him."[14]

Even if we grant that greatness is not identical with goodness, it does not follow that pure, unadulterated evil is an irrelevant consideration. Was Hitler an evil Bismarck, or a cunning and reckless adventurer whose opponents were so paralyzed by the thought of another and more terrible European war that they refined the art of appeasement? Once confronted, the Führer displayed appalling judgment, even from the practical point of view. Stalin? He was a gangster and mass murderer. As for his "statesmanship": "it was," Kennan observed, "the protection of his personal position that came first; and this was the key to his diplomacy."[15] No one could say that of Bismarck, the model of a great statesman. One can only conclude that, in this case, Kennan allowed the two tyrants' successes to affect his judgment. He forgot that greatness is a function of character, not success.

To be sure, in his lectures Kennan was sharply critical of Stalin's diplomacy, and of Soviet diplomacy in general. At the same time, however, he had few words of praise for American and Western policymakers. In general, he disapproved of any departure from diplomacy that was conducted in private by professionals and that regarded the national interest as the sole criterion when making decisions. He thought poorly of what came to be called summit diplomacy, in part because it was too public and propagandistic, in part because heads of state were burdened with so many responsibilities that they could not devote the necessary attention to any particular problem or issue. He saw little evidence that Western statesmen possessed the ability to view things from the perspectives of others—a result of "a certain parochialism of the Anglo-Saxon mind, and particularly the American mind." Nor were they able to abandon "universalistic and messianic pretensions" and to concede the principle of live-and-let-live in relations between states.[16]

◆◆◆

In his lectures on World War II, Kennan argued that the West should not have allowed itself to believe that the Soviets were allies out of friendship or some commonality of interest. Western leaders should have made it clear to Stalin that they would aid the Russian cause only as long and insofar as it served their interests. It was not in their interest, he maintained, to insist upon unconditional surrender—this rigid demand guaranteed that the Soviets would extend their empire into Eastern Europe. Kennan conceded that no useful purpose would have been served by negotiating with Hitler, but he reminded his students of the German resistance, for which, as we have seen, he reserved a profound sympathy.

With Moltke very much in mind, he said that the resistance "was composed of men who were very brave and very lonely, and were so much closer to us in feeling and in ideals than they were to either Hitler or Stalin that the difference between them and us paled, comparatively, into insignificance." He knew, on the basis of personal experience, that those courageous men had received no encouragement from the Allies. In fact, the policy of unconditional surrender "implied that Germany would be treated with equal severity whether or not Hitler was overthrown," and this "cut the ground out from under any moderate German opposition."[17]

Later in the same lecture, Kennan reiterated his belief that a distinction had always to be made between ruler and ruled. He made clear his hostility to Nazism and all its works but insisted that Roosevelt and Churchill had been too ready to tar all Germans with the Nazi brush. They could not liberate themselves from the prejudices of World War I and believed, tragically and mistakenly, that they were fighting some deeply ingrained German conservatism, when it was precisely the German conservatives who recognized the dishonor that Hitler had brought upon their country, who organized resistance to Nazi rule, and who—many of them—sacrificed their lives.

In the final chapter of his book, Kennan warned against any thought of a regime change in Russia, especially one effected by military force. Outright war, he argued, was too undiscriminating a device for such a change; too many innocents would die. Moreover, however much a people might wish to be relieved of a repressive regime, they wished even less to be subjected to the destruction and hardship of modern wars. Then too, however despotic a ruler, his position of power gave him, "as Gibbon once pointed out, a certain identity of interest with those who are ruled."[18]

Kennan concluded his lectures—and his book—by stating what he understood to be the lessons of his analyses of Russian-Western relations. Chief among them was "the necessity of an American outlook which accepts the obligations of maturity and consents to operate in a world of relative and unstable values."[19] This was not the best of all imaginable worlds, but it was—though Kennan did not use these words—the best of all *possible* worlds.

Early in 1959, Kennan set down some reflections on his experience at Oxford; intended for the *Times* of London, they never found their way into print—which is a pity. "I am alarmed," he wrote, "at the prevailing absence not only of a conscious faith but even of any visible interest in religion among a people the foundations of whose greatness rested on the bedrock of the Christian Church; and conversely, at the prevalence of what struck me as an uncritical spirit of egalitarianism and materialism." What he found pleasing were little things such as the reverberation of the chimes of the Merton College chapel through the street below, the half-frozen footpaths along the Thames, and the gentility of an old seaside hotel.[20] Such simple pleasures were, in his view, underappreciated; they gave to life its distinctive flavor.

Kennan devoted six chapters of *Russia and the West* to the Treaty of Brest-Litovsk and the Allied interventions in north Russia and Siberia. He did so not only because these were pivotal events at the dawn of the Soviet-American relationship but because he had just completed his first scholarly work—a two-volume history titled *Soviet-American Relations, 1917–1920* (1956–58). Each volume ran to more than five hundred pages because, Kennan told his readers, events always resulted from a great many decisions and actions of a great many people. "The acts and decisions of statesmanship," he wrote in the preface to the first volume, "will seldom be found entirely intelligible if viewed apart from the immediate context of time and circumstance—information, associates, pressures, prejudices, impulses, and momentary necessities—in which they occur."[21]

But in fact there was another reason why Kennan wrote at such length: his fear that he would be criticized by professionals, including colleagues at the institute, for superficiality and insufficient research—that, he told the British historian Herbert Butterfield, was the principal reason for the "appalling accumulation of detail."[22]

Kennan's award-winning history reflected its author's belief, which we have already noted, that the past held valuable lessons for the present. More than a superb re-creation of the tangled events of the past, it was a devastating critique of American foreign policy, and of those most responsible for its conduct. The principal figure, of course, was President Woodrow Wilson, a former professor who had once served as president of Kennan's alma mater. Kennan wrote of Wilson with respect and a proper appreciation for the burdens imposed by the nation's highest office. He gave the president due credit for his principled opposition to intervention in Russia's internal politics. Nevertheless, he portrayed him as the embodiment of much that was wrong with American foreign policy, including an inability to understand "that the political principles by which [Americans] lived might have been historically conditioned and might not enjoy universal validity."[23]

Because Kennan believed the Great War to have been the great catastrophe of modern Western civilization, he could not but be highly critical of Wilson's decision to enter the United States into the fray. Not only was this a significant departure from the historic policy of avoiding entangling alliances, but it led the president, in trying to rally the nation, to cast the war in ideological and absolutist terms. Thanks to the collapse of tsarist rule in Russia, he could advertise the war as a decisive struggle between democracy and absolutism, a war to make the world safe for democracy. This proclaimed purpose made it difficult, if not impossible, to settle for anything short of total victory.

Not long after U.S. entry into the war, the provisional government that had assumed power when the tsar could no longer compel obedience fell to a Bolshevik coup orchestrated by Lenin and Trotsky. Among the new regime's initial steps was an appeal to the Germans for an armistice, leading to a separate peace. Such a peace, quite naturally, would have presented a serious problem for the Allies, for it would have allowed the Germans to shift large numbers of troops to the western front.

What ought the U.S. attitude be toward Soviet power? Much would depend, not only in the period 1917–20 but subsequently, upon how that question was answered. Unfortunately, as Kennan pointed out, Wilson had never been in Russia and possessed little knowledge of Russian affairs. As someone committed to universal democracy, he had felt distaste for tsarist autocracy and sympathy for the revolutionary movement, but to understand the differences between the Bolsheviks and other revolutionary groups such as the Mensheviks and the Social Revolutionaries (SRs) was quite beyond his capacity.

Even more important, according to Kennan, was Wilson's disinclination to rely upon the counsel of professional diplomats or to pursue his objectives by means of traditional diplomatic methods. If he sought any advice at all, it was from his confidant Colonel Edward M. House, not from David Francis, whom he had named ambassador to Russia in 1916. To be sure, Francis was not a professional diplomat, but a political appointee who had previously served as mayor of St. Louis, governor of Missouri, and secretary of the interior under Grover Cleveland. Given his lack of preparation and experience, his age (he turned sixty-five in 1916), and his modest abilities, Francis did what he could, and Kennan accorded him proper respect. He pointed out, for example, that his assignment was made more difficult by the policy (which, however, he supported) of nonrecognition of the Bolshevik regime, decided upon in December 1917 in part because the Bolsheviks were not democrats, in part because they sought to withdraw from the war.

Kennan believed that decision to have been a mistake—a result of "the characteristic American concept of diplomatic representation as a gesture of friendship to peoples rather than

75

a channel of communication among governments."[24] It was already clear, he argued, that Soviet power was a reality, and however distasteful that reality might be, it was in the national interest to keep open some avenue of communication. This, for somewhat different reasons, was also the view of Raymond Robins, head of a Red Cross mission to Russia who took it upon himself to act as a kind of semi-official diplomat.

About Robins, Kennan had a great deal to say. The adventurous American had discovered gold in Alaska and then, from some feeling of guilt or responsibility, had developed a social conscience. Before going to Russia, he had helped to found the Progressive Party and chaired its 1916 convention in Chicago. Thanks in large measure to his constant companion, Alexander Gumberg (born Michael Gruzenberg), a Soviet citizen—and, according to William Bullitt, a communist agent who took orders from Lenin and Trotsky[25]—Robins was able to move freely in high Bolshevik circles.

Along with British diplomat Bruce Lockhart and French Captain Jacques Sadoul, Robins was greatly taken with the Bolshevik leaders. Trotsky, he once remarked, was "a four kind son of a bitch, but the greatest Jew since Christ."[26] Kennan insisted that Robins was not a communist sympathizer; perhaps not, but he did have a rather starry-eyed view of what was, from the beginning, an undisguised despotism. In any event, it was Robins's belief in the necessity of contact with the Soviet authorities that earned him Kennan's approval.

Unfortunately, in Kennan's view, Robins was also the kind of irregular diplomat whom Washington should have discouraged. It was always unwise, he believed, to permit inexperienced people, whose status was unclear, to dabble in transactions between governments. That is one reason why he chose not to dedicate the second volume of his history, *The Decision to Intervene,* to Robins but to the memory of Dewitt Clinton Poole and Maddin Summers, two members of America's foreign service of "whose faithful and distinguished efforts in Russia on their country's behalf this volume gives only an incomplete account."[27]

Poole and Summers both tried to make the best of a difficult situation that was made worse by lack of guidance from Washington and confusion with respect to seats of authority. Both found themselves caught up in the tragic drama that was the Allied intervention. The story of the intervention is a complicated one, and Kennan told it well. He was concerned above all to make two major points: that the intervention was a costly mistake, and that the United States, despite later charges by Soviet historians, played a reluctant and minor role—and one that related primarily to the prosecution of the war.

After Russia exited the war in March 1918, the Allies worried that war supplies in Archangel and Vladivostok, supplies that they had provided, might fall into German hands, with or without Bolshevik collaboration. Fearing an attack on Murmansk—site of a new and relatively ice-free port not far distant from Archangel—by Finns under German command, a small British and French force went ashore in March. The Murmansk Soviet was dominated by Mensheviks and SRs and pursued an independent course not unfriendly to the Allies; it offered no objection. What Kennan could not have known is that Lenin and Stalin initially approved of the Allied landing for fear of losing the port to the German-Finnish force.[28] Bolsheviks in control of Vladivostok did object, however, to the party of Japanese marines that landed in April after the murder on shore of three of their countrymen. The British promptly sent some fifty men to protect their consulate.

These were small and defensible actions—hardly an intervention that had as its aim the overthrow of Soviet power. But matters took a different turn as a result of the so-called Czech Legion. Originally made up of Russian-born Czechs and Slovaks, the legion had received permission from the provisional government to open its ranks to Czech and Slovak POWs. By the end of 1917, it numbered sixty thousand men and constituted a formidable fighting force that was hostile to the Central Powers and especially to Austria-Hungary. The Allies therefore recognized them and placed them under the French High Command. Thanks to negotiations with Thomas Masaryk, who was working for "Czechoslovak" independence, the Soviets granted the legion permission to move across Siberia to Vladivostok, whence Allied ships were to transport it around the world to France, where it would join in the struggle against the Germans.

Before long, however, Trotsky, who had not been party to the original negotiations, demanded that all noncommunist Russian officers attached to the legion be removed and that the Czechs retain only enough arms to defend themselves. Increasingly suspicious, the Czechs hid their arms and used them when, after a violent clash with some Hungarian prisoners, they turned on local Soviet authorities investigating the incident. Trotsky then issued a characteristic order: "Every armed Czechoslovak found on the railway is to be shot on the spot."[29] On May 26, 1918, hostilities between the Czechs and the Bolsheviks broke out all along the Trans-Siberian Railroad line.

Rather than have the Czechs shoot their way through to Vladivostok, the British, and eventually the French, thought they had a better idea: use them, in conjunction with a Japanese intervention, to reopen the eastern front. The Japanese, though eager to intervene in their own interest, wished first to gain American approval, but Wilson remained unconvinced concerning the prospects for a new front and was in any case opposed to interventions—at least until he met Masaryk, who was, like him, a professor and a believer in democracy as a kind of secular religion. He represented, moreover, a small people of the kind for which Wilson reserved a special sympathy.

On July 6, 1918, Wilson called a White House meeting of his top advisors and set forth a series of propositions and a program of action. Having learned that the Czechs had succeeded in taking Vladivostok, he stated that the U.S. and other governments were obligated to help them form a junction with their compatriots farther to the west. He therefore proposed the sending of seven thousand troops to Vladivostok, where they would join the same number of Japanese troops. The combined force would guard the Czechs' line of communication as they moved west. The U.S. and Japan would announce publicly that their only purpose was to aid the Czechs in their fight against German and Austrian prisoners.

As Kennan pointed out, however, it was the Bolsheviks, not German and Austrian prisoners, who were the Czechs' opponents and who would be able to exploit the intervention for propaganda purposes. In the end, the Americans achieved nothing of value and lost whatever possibility there was—Kennan thought it small but real—of limited communication with the Bolshevik regime, communication that might have altered the subsequent course of Soviet-American relations. In April 1920, the last American troops withdrew; the Japanese, who had joined the battle in far greater numbers than originally planned, followed in the fall of 1922.

Kennan did not believe that America's blunders in Russia, 1917–20, were peculiar to that time and place. They were rooted in a strange and disturbing immaturity that seemed to have gripped the national character. For one thing, Americans had convinced themselves that they had discovered *the* principles by which other peoples ought to order their public lives. They could not seem to grasp the fact that those principles were products of a particular historical experience. Americans were universalists in a world of relativities—the world of political and social arrangements.

Believing in inevitable progress, Americans were bewildered by the death and destruction that the Great War brought about. Such things, they reasoned, could not be attributed to some flaw in human nature; they must have been foisted upon the rest of us by the beastlike "Huns." The war could be regarded as a struggle between good and evil, everything German being tainted. "The treatment," Kennan wrote of the war years, "of 'hyphenated-Americans' and people with German names was cruel, undiscriminating, and often wholly disgraceful."[30] He was right.

Kennan's critique sheds light on his own deeply held beliefs. He believed that ours is, and will remain, an imperfect world, and, like Dewitt Poole, he maintained a "cheerful" skepticism regarding human nature. That being the case, he had no use for utopian projects—he mentioned Lenin specifically—that embraced a

> violent and total break with the past, the virtual destruction of man's social and political heritage, the unlimited belief in the power of contemporary man to understand his own problems and to chart his own course, the centralization of all social and political authority, the subordination of all local and individual impulses to collective purpose, centrally defined, and the deliberate destruction of large elements of humanity in the interests of a predicted progress of the remainder.[31]

He looked, rather,

> to ethical standards—largely religious in origin—as the foundation of all human progress; accepted as relevant to contemporary problems the wisdom and experience of former generations; believed that change, to be useful, must be gradual, organic, and non-destructive; . . . and preferred, generally, to bear with the imperfections of so-

ciety . . . hoping that they could be gradually and gently bent to a better shape, rather than attempt to uproot and destroy them all at once, at the risk of uprooting and destroying God knows what else.[32]

I have quoted Kennan at some length not only because of the eloquence of his prose but because of the profound conservatism that it reflects. Based upon his assessment of man's strengths and weaknesses, limits and possibilities, he had concluded that no people is so superior that it can treat others as lesser beings, no political system so perfect that all others must embrace it. In public as well as private life, a sense of proportion, of modesty, of restraint, of one's own failings was imperative.

From these first works of scholarship, Kennan had learned that the studying and writing of history was a lonely occupation, one that tended to cut one off from one's own time. He had already learned too what he told members of the American Academy of Arts and Letters in 1986—that every work of history "is at least as revealing of the man who wrote it and the period in which it was written as it is of the people it portrays and the époque in which they lived."[33] That was certainly true of *Soviet-American Relations, 1917–1920.* The work was obviously written during the era of the Cold War, when the Soviet-American relationship was not simply of historical interest. Kennan was, for example, at considerable pains to show that Soviet histories of the Allied intervention grossly misrepresented America's purposes and exaggerated the extent of her involvement.

More important, the work revealed much about Kennan himself. When, for example, he wrote of his forebear George Kennan, he projected a self-image: "Quiet, gentlemanly, moderate but always clear and forceful in his language, conservative as an American though a friend of liberalism in Russia, the protagonist of no particular ideology but merely the advocate of compassion, decency, and tolerance in the adjustment of political differences within Russia."[34] This *was* a fair description of Kennan himself, though he would have been justified in adding "possessed of a melancholic temperament."

The latter characteristic is perhaps most on display in the diary entries that Kennan made during his travels. Having completed his year at Oxford he returned to Princeton, but he continued to seize every opportunity—the summer months, international conferences—to move about the world. Consider, for example, his account of an afternoon's excursion in Denmark in June 1958. On a local train he watches as a passenger disappears down the station platform "and out of my life . . . a tiny wrench and a tiny parting—a symbol of the underlying impermanence and loneliness of the human state."[35]

In September of the following year, he is in Hamburg and laments the fact that the Europe of his youth is no more. This prompts him to reflect that while we are living longer, the pace of change deprives us of the only world we are able to understand and in which we can orient ourselves. "We older people are the guests of this age, permitted to haunt its strange and somewhat terrifying halls—in a way part of its life, like the guests in a summer hotel, yet in a similar way detached from it."[36]

In June 1960, a year before the wall went up, Kennan is in Berlin. One evening he and a friend drive into the East, where they chance upon the ruins of the Wilhelmian Romanesque cathedral. East Berlin was then filled with ruins and bombed-out areas, in stark contrast to bustling, booming West Berlin. And yet it is to the ruins that Kennan is drawn; he glimpses in them a certain grandeur. "There was a stillness, a beauty, a sense of infinite, elegiac sadness and timelessness such as I have never experienced." He sees three boys sitting quietly on the steps leading to what is left of the cathedral; to him they are "the embodiment of man's lost and purposeless state, his loneliness, his helplessness, his wistfulness, and his inability to understand."[37]

That fall John F. Kennedy won election to the presidency. Among the first things the young chief executive did after assuming office was to phone Kennan, who was then leading a graduate seminar at Yale, to offer him appointment as ambassador to Poland or Yugoslavia. In a matter of hours the former ambassador to the Soviet Union, eager for a fresh challenge, accepted the Yugoslav post. "I am happy to be back in the thick of things," he told the Associated Press. "I liked the academic life, but I became tired and stale writing in solitude. I missed diplomacy."[38]

The choice of Yugoslavia was easy to make because Kennan believed that the Yugoslav defection from the Soviet bloc had been a blow to the Soviets precisely because it raised the question as to whether monolithic unity and discipline were essential to the development of Marxism: whether one could not be a good communist without taking orders from Moscow and without following slavishly the pattern of institutions and methods established by the Soviet Union. After rather hurried preparation, he, his wife, and their two youngest children set out for Europe aboard an ocean liner; they arrived in Belgrade in early May 1961.

On a personal level, Kennan enjoyed his tour of duty in the fascinating multiethnic Balkan land. By the 1960s, Marshal Tito had moderated his dictatorship and was pursuing a neutral policy as between the two Great Powers. Kennan did not feel, as he had in the USSR, harassed or restricted in any way. Quite the contrary—he moved about the country without hindrance. This time his greatest problem was with his own country. Too many members of Congress, most of whom were grossly ignorant of Eastern European affairs, viewed Yugoslavia as just another communist country and opposed trade because they confused it with aid. With their eyes fixed upon domestic politics, they were determined to establish their credentials as staunch anticommunists.

Kennan was apoplectic when word reached him that Congress planned to bar the extension of any and all aid to Yugoslavia, even though virtually all aid had already come to an end. Worse still, members intended to deny the country most-favored-nation status. Against these senseless and counterproductive steps, Kennan protested vigorously. What was the point, he asked, of destroying reasonably good relations and driving Belgrade back into the arms of Moscow?

No one offered a satisfactory answer to that question. In its wisdom, Congress did pass a bill refusing Yugoslavia most-favored-nation treatment; much to Kennan's disappointment, President Kennedy signed the bill into law. When that happened, he knew that his usefulness was at an end; the Yugoslavs might respect him personally but they could not fail to recognize that his views carried no weight at home. The time had come to think about his future. He had, he told Oppenheimer, received offers to teach at Princeton, Tufts, Harvard, and Yale; should he accept one of them or should he devote himself to the writing of history? If he did enter academic life on a full-time basis, he feared that he would be under constant pressure to focus his attention on current events and, as a result, fail to produce any work of permanent value. On the personal side, his wife, he said, wished to remain in Princeton, and he himself disliked the idea of pulling up stakes, not least because he felt a deep attachment to the institute.[39]

Kennan stayed on in Belgrade as a lame duck until July 1963—and then returned to the institute, where he looked forward to resuming his writing. Before settling down to work, he wrote to Marshal Tito to express his "respect and admiration."[40] Kennan tended to judge foreign leaders by the way in which they dealt with other countries, particularly the United States, not by the way in which they governed at home. This habit, together with the personal good relations he established with the Yugoslav dictator, is almost certainly why he was excessively uncritical, though one should also keep in mind that Tito, by the time Kennan arrived on the scene, had evolved into a leader more authoritarian than totalitarian.

Kennan's career in the foreign service of his country was now definitely at an end, and he felt such a profound sense of relief that he decided to purchase a 32-foot Norwegian "motor-sailor," the "Nagawicka" (after the Wisconsin lake where he spent summers as a boy). The acquisition responded to "some deep psychic need"; it was "a symbol of personal freedom—of liberation, or potential liberation, from a mainland life that seemed without hopeful prospects." It offered an escape "from the strains of representation—of pretending, for good and useful reason, to be what one was really not." Such strains "gave no release to the real person inside."[41]

Not long after Kennan settled back into life in Princeton, Lee Harvey Oswald assassinated President Kennedy, an event that may be said to mark the beginning of the historical—as opposed to the chronological—"sixties," years of upheaval that exposed some of the vulnerabilities of Western civilization. Living near a university campus, Kennan was particularly struck and disturbed by student radicalism. When invited to give a brief speech at the dedication of a new library at Swarthmore College, he used the occasion to warn of the danger posed by young people who reminded him of Russia's revolutionary Populists of the nineteenth century. "It was out of just such radical students, frustrated in their efforts to help the Russian peasant, that Lenin forged his highly disciplined faction. It was in part from people of just this desperate and confused state of mind that Hitler recruited his supporters."[42]

Why was it, he wondered aloud, that young people hungry for revolutionary action remained on campus, a place, at least in the traditional understanding, of semi-monastic withdrawal, the purpose of which was to reflect calmly upon life in its more permanent aspects? He suspected, quite rightly, that their presence on campus was dictated by a fear that they would be conscripted and sent to Vietnam and an awareness that campuses served as rallying points and havens of permissiveness.

Kennan distinguished between angry and violent militants who exhibited an extraordinary degree of certainty concerning their own rectitude and the iniquity of those with whom they disagreed, and hippies who believed that peace could be achieved by "making love, not war" and that drugs would release hitherto unsuspected and untapped human powers. Drawing upon his greater experience of life and the world, he warned the young, for most of whom history had become "irrelevant," that past utopian efforts to bring heaven to earth had done far more harm than humble efforts to bring a little order and civility to one's own immediate surroundings. And in a provocative challenge to the students' conventional wisdom, he declared that "the decisive seat of evil in this world is not in social and political institutions . . . but simply in the weakness and imperfection of the human soul itself."[43]

When, on January 21, 1968, the New York Times published Kennan's remarks under the title "Rebels Without a Program," all hell broke loose. Incensed students and their equally irate defenders deluged editors and Kennan himself with letters of protest. In many of them, young men complained bitterly of the draft, though not one mentioned fear as a reason for his indignation; it was only, they wished Kennan to believe, their unwillingness to violate their conscience by participating in an unjust war. The undoubted plight of black Americans, the alleged evils of the military and corporations, and the moral compromises said to have been made by older generations were also subjected to relentless criticism.

Almost everything that Kennan had said came under attack. "Every fiber of my being," a Notre Dame senior wrote, "every holy and intimate experience I have known cries out against" the idea that the source of evil lies within each of us. Improved institutions, a member of Columbia's Students for a Democratic Society (SDS) insisted, could make "war and poverty, exploitation and racism" disappear. Contrary to what Kennan had averred, another added, "much of the creative and constructive thought of our age has been facilitated by drug experience" (unfortunately for his argument, he cited the music of John Lennon). There was nothing wrong with self-indulgence, a Harvard graduate informed Kennan, so long as it hurt no one else. Kennan's call for abnegation, order, and physical cleanliness had, he said, an ominous ring. "It is sad that Kennan does not realize that Hitler might well have used the same words."[44]

After reading every letter and making extensive notes, Kennan wrote a long reply to his critics; more than a mere defense of his speech, however, the reply articulated a social and political philosophy that was worthy of Edmund Burke (whom, along with Gibbon, Kennan mentioned favorably). He expressed his deep regret that the letters bespoke such unhappiness; if they were any indication, the student radicals lacked any *joie de vivre*. Tense and defiant, they seemed completely ignorant of the fact that life could be made more enjoyable, and even more socially useful, by cultivating the amenities.

That young radicals were relentless in their pursuit of various mass-emotional causes there could be no doubt, but Kennan asked whether it was really the misery of others that troubled them. Was their outrage at injustices, real and imagined, not "the expression of some inner need, to which the objects have only a casual relevance?" If the war in Vietnam should end and the draft be eliminated, would these restless youths not remain on the prowl for causes? The questions were meant to be rhetorical, because Kennan believed that student radicals were the products "of the sickly secularism of [American] society, of the appalling shallowness of the religious, philosophic and political concepts that pervade it."[45] Deprived by secularization of any sense of purpose or meaning, they experienced a profound discontent that could be alleviated only by discovering, or creating for themselves, some reason to live.

Kennan felt a genuine sympathy for their predicament, but he was not prepared to let their claims and charges go unchallenged. He began by restating his own outspoken opposition to the war in Vietnam. A month after the *New York Times* published "Rebels Without a Program," he had departed from his customary aloofness from electoral politics in order to introduce Senator Eugene McCarthy at a dinner to support the senator's presidential candidacy. He knew that McCarthy's political hero was Adlai Stevenson, whose presidential candidacies he had also supported publicly; more important, he admired McCarthy's courage in challenging President Lyndon Johnson for the Democratic nomination, largely on a platform of opposition to the war in Vietnam.

Kennan thought it vitally important that the war be ended. No conceivable political outcome to the conflict, he had told those gathered, "could justify the attendant suffering and destruction." Moreover, while national attention remained focused on a remote corner of the world, serious problems at home were largely neglected.[46]

Nevertheless, Kennan now made it clear to his critics that there could be instances in which a communist seizure of power would be a proper concern of American statesmen; that the Vietnamese communists were guilty of the worst kind of brutality; and that *they* had provoked actions on the Americans' part that resulted in civilian suffering. Opposition to the draft was, Kennan pointed out, unmodified by any sense of obligation to the country—under any circumstances. Pious declarations of pacifism left him unmoved; his objection to that particular form of self-righteousness deserves quotation in full not only because of the cogency of his argument but because of the power of his prose.

> The central function of government, as I see it, is the as-
> surance of the public order. This is something for which
> nobody has ever found any suitable means that do not in-
> clude, at some point, the devices of coercion. This is true
> of the democracy as it is of the dictatorship. Whoever re-
> lies on these devices—on the police and the courts and
> the prisons—as instruments for the assurance of his own
> protection and his own enjoyment of civil rights—has
> no moral basis, as I see it, for denying his contribution to
> their maintenance. The same applies to the arrangements
> for the national defense. No one has a moral right to deny
> on principle his contribution to this part of our national
> life . . . unless he is really prepared to commit its destinies
> to the good graces of an extremely jealous and largely hos-
> tile outside world.[47]

As much as he detested violence, Kennan exhibited little patience for those, like the Quakers, who seemed unable to understand that man's demonic side could ultimately be restrained
only by force. "Violence," he once explained to the Friends, "is
the tribute we pay to original sin."[48]

In his remarks at Swarthmore, Kennan had maintained that,
in a democracy, civil disobedience could never be justified, but
a thoughtful letter from W. H. Auden caused him to rethink his
position—or rather to refine it. A distinction should be made—
here he conceded Auden's point—between legitimate defiance

when confronted with state efforts to compel actions on the part of an individual who views them as morally unacceptable and lawlessness taken up as a protest against general actions of the state deemed to be unjust. Without in any way minimizing the importance of justice, Kennan maintained that, given "the primitive chaos of [men's] souls,"[49] order was the higher value. In the priority he thus granted to order, the emphasis he placed upon the need for restraint, and the appreciation he showed for every effort to lift men above animal existence, Kennan associated himself with the conservative tradition.

◆◆◆

Kennan's confrontation with student radicals left on him an indelible mark. He had for some time maintained that the greatest threat faced by the United States and the West in general was not external, not Soviet aggression, but internal, the weakening of individual self-discipline and the erosion of public standards of conduct. Of this he was now even more certain. Some years later, in a famous letter addressed to *Die Zeit* in Hamburg, he had this to say.

> Poor old West: succumbing feebly, day by day, to its own decadence, sliding into debility on the slime of its own self-indulgent permissiveness; its drugs, its crime, its pornography, its pampering of the youth, its addiction to its bodily comforts, its rampant materialism and consumerism—and then trembling before the menace of the wicked Russians, all pictured as supermen, eight feet tall, their internal problems all essentially solved, and with nothing else now to think about except how to bring damage and destruction to Western Europe. This persistent externalization of the sense of danger—this persistent exaggera- ·

tion of the threat from without and blindness to the threat from within: this is the symptom of some deep failure to come to terms with reality—and with one's self.[50]

It should come as no surprise, then, that Kennan seized the opportunity to spend several months of 1969 out of the United States as a visiting fellow at All Souls College, Oxford. While there he was invited to deliver the annual Chichele Lectures and chose as his subject the Marquis de Custine's *La Russie en 1839,* suggested to him by a work of another French aristocrat with which he was most familiar: Alexis de Tocqueville's *Democracy in America.* The two men had much in common, though Kennan judged Custine, as a literary figure, to be the greater. The success of the lectures encouraged him to turn them into a small book, which Princeton University Press published in 1971.

Kennan did not pass over the fact that Custine was a notorious homosexual, but he treated the matter with delicacy, in part out of kindness but also because, in matters of judgment, he often sympathized with the Marquis. Custine too wanted to earn a place for himself among the better writers of his time. He was, Kennan recognized, a man of the eighteenth century, a confirmed elitist and anti-egalitarian. And yet, as a direct result of his travels in Russia, he had become a defender of representative government as the form best adapted to preserve "the people on the one side from democratic license, and on the other, from the most glaring abuses of despotism."[51]

This was precisely Kennan's view as well. In his reply to radical students, he had first dismissed the charge, made by some of them, that the government of the United States was totalitarian. Speaking as one who, unlike them, had lived in Hitler's Germany and Stalin's Russia, he maintained that anyone making such a claim knew not the meaning of the word. He admitted, however, to concern about the direct intervention of "the people" in the workings of government. The parliamentary institution, however imperfect, was in his view an indispensable link between the will of the people and the exercise of governmental authority.

Kennan also admired Custine's preference for a small state that concentrated on the internal improvement of its own society—as opposed to a large state determined to expand its power. In his reply to radical students, he had stated his belief "that our country is too large for its own good. Great countries . . . are a menace to themselves and everyone else. People are not meant to live in such vast, impersonal political communities."[52] Above all, however, Kennan praised Custine for recognizing that Russia's strength was always a function of Europe's weakness. That was as true in the present as it was in the past. Before worrying about the Russian bear and stockpiling more nuclear weapons, the peoples of the West would do well to concentrate their efforts on putting their own houses in order.

Despite his sympathy for many of the Marquis' views, Kennan conceded that Custine's literary portrait of Nicholas I's Russia was deeply flawed. He had made numerous errors of fact, and his entire outlook was colored by what he had been told by Polish emigrés in Paris, rabidly anti-Russian to the man. At the same time, he argued that the book offered valuable insights into Stalin's Russia—with respect, for example, to the absolute power of one man, the paranoid fear of espionage, and the obsession with secrecy. There was much truth in this. Nicholas was assuredly not Stalin, and his repressions, while certainly real, never rose to the level of terror—under which there is no necessary relationship between one's acts and the consequences of those acts. Tsarism, in a word, was not Bolshevism.

Kennan emphasized this fact by pointing out that Custine, though he grasped the nature of autocratic rule and even apprehended dimly certain revolutionary tendencies, remained blind to the existence and future importance of Russian liberalism. Between 1839 and 1914, that liberalism, for which Kennan had enormous respect, brought about large and meaningful changes in Russian life. He mentioned, among other things, the abolition of serfdom, the laying of foundations for local self-government, the reform of the judicial system, and the creation of a parliament, however limited in power. Had the Great War not interrupted the process of liberal evolution, there was every reason to believe that Russia would have joined the community of Western nations.

Without the war, the Bolsheviks would not have come to power. History was, Kennan asserted once again, radically contingent. It was a reasonable view, he insisted,

> (this writer, among others, adheres to it) that the Russian Revolution was fortuitous, insofar as it was the product of a number of factors in the sudden coming-together of which no logical pattern can be discerned. One can think of a number of individual circumstances any one of which might very easily, but for the hand of chance, have been quite different than it actually was—and different in such a way as to obviate the second Russian Revolution of 1917, if not the first.[53]

It was with historical contingency in mind that Kennan set to work on the origins of World War I, the event that lay at the heart of the "decline of this Western civilization."[54] Communism in Russia, Nazism in Germany, World War II, the Cold War—all, in his view, were products of the disaster of 1914–18. Because he believed that the war was not inevitable, he was determined to discover what went wrong—not simply out of scholarly curiosity but in the hope of guiding the decisions of contemporary statesmen and educating their peoples so as to prevent another, truly apocalyptic, conflict.

But how to accomplish his task? Like almost every historian working on the recent past, Kennan was overwhelmed by the sheer volume of available source material. He knew that at his age—he turned seventy in 1974—he lacked the time and stamina to master it all, or even the greater part of it. And in any case, he did not intend to write a sprawling work that, by its very comprehensiveness, would make it difficult if not impossible for readers to grasp its lessons. He decided, therefore, to write a "micro-history" that would isolate a smaller sector of events and show in detail how and why men acted as they did, how it was that they stumbled, blindly, into the abyss.

Even in the knowledge that European diplomatic history had fallen into academic disfavor, Kennan chose to focus his attention on the diplomatic background to the war; as a result of his own career in the foreign service, he had learned a great deal about successful and unsuccessful diplomacy, about how to distinguish between the national interest and impulses of a reckless and dangerous kind. He had a command of French, German, and Russian, and he had gained, over the years, a profound understanding of the Russian mind and character. The choice of subject therefore presented itself insistently: he would investigate Franco-Russian relations leading up to and following the fateful alliance of 1894.

The era that Kennan planned to study opened with the pivotal events of the years 1864–71: the unification of Germany, the exclusion of Austria from the new reich, and the defeat of France by Prussia. The central figure in all of these events was, of course, the great Prussian statesman Otto von Bismarck. For that consummate realist, Kennan had nothing but respect and admiration. In a time of romantic nationalism, Bismarck remained an old-fashioned—according to Kennan, an eighteenth-century—Prussian patriot. Unmoved by nationalism or any other ideology and unshaken by the nineteenth century's nervous instability, he made Prussia's national interest his lodestar.

True, he provoked, fought, and won three wars between 1864 and 1871, but he always projected concrete and realistic *political* objectives. Once having achieved those objectives, he made an end to hostilities; never was he tempted by imperialistic dreams or by a desire to see his enemies destroyed. In fact, he did not regard them as "enemies," but as momentary obstacles to his plan to solidify his country's security. To him "Germany" was simply a Greater Prussia, one better able to deter aggression; his duty was to restore as quickly as possible good relations with those states—especially Austria and France—that had been humbled by Prussian arms.

With Austria—after 1867, Austria-Hungary—Bismarck successfully negotiated an alliance in 1879. It provided for mutual support in the event that either party should be attacked by Russia or a power allied with Russia. Should France alone attack Germany, Austria-Hungary was merely to maintain a benevolent neutrality. France presented a more difficult problem, not least because Bismarck had, somewhat reluctantly and for strategic reasons, taken Alsace and Lorraine. Kennan believed this to have been one of the master diplomat's few mistakes, though, like Bismarck himself, he doubted whether France's desire for revenge would have been any the less intense had the two provinces been permitted to remain French. Confident that France would, without having a strong ally, hesitate before risking a war of *revanche,* Bismarck recognized the importance of maintaining good relations with Russia—in that way avoiding the danger of a Franco-Russian military alliance and a war on two fronts.

Having served as Prussian ambassador in Russia, Bismarck had concluded that Prussia had no fundamental interests in conflict with those of Russia. Russian friendship, then, could be purchased for a minimal price. Especially was this true when one recalled that Tsar Alexander II revered his uncle, Kaiser Wilhelm I. Trouble between the two countries brewed, however, in the wake of the Russian-Turkish War of 1877–78. Neither Austria-Hungary nor England was prepared to accept the Russian-imposed Treaty of San Stefano (March 3, 1878), which provided for Russian occupation of a vast Bulgaria with a seaboard on the Aegean. The Austro-Hungarian Foreign Minister, Count Gyula Andrássy, called for a congress of the powers to meet in Berlin.

Bismarck presided at the Congress of Berlin (1878) as, in his words, an "honest broker." As a result of the decisions made there (actually, the Russians had already signed an agreement with England), a far smaller Bulgaria (37.5 percent of the size of the San Stefano state) was divided into two parts: Bulgaria proper (north of the Balkan Mountains) to be a principality under nominal Turkish suzerainty, and "Eastern Rumelia" (south of the Balkans) to be governed by a Christian appointed by the sultan. Bosnia and Herzegovina, which had risen against Ottoman rule in 1875—helping to trigger the Russian declaration of war against Turkey—were to be occupied and administered by Austria-Hungary. This was clearly an effort to foil Russian, particularly Pan-Slav, ambitions with respect to the Balkans and the straits of the Bosporus and Dardanelles.

The Russians, having suffered a diplomatic defeat, even a humiliation, placed much of the blame on Bismarck, whose true objective was to establish Russian and Austro-Hungarian spheres of influence in the Balkans and thus to reduce the danger of war. Another way to do that was to renew the Dreikaiserbund (Three Emperors' League) of 1872–73. Agreed to in secret in 1881, the league committed Austria-Hungary, Germany, and Russia to benevolent neutrality if one of them found itself at war with a fourth power (excluding Turkey). Austria-Hungary gained the right to annex Bosnia and Herzegovina when it saw fit, and the three powers agreed not to stand in the way of an eventual union of Bulgaria and Eastern Rumelia.

The conclusion of negotiations was delayed somewhat by the assassination in March 1881 of Tsar Alexander II. The new tsar, Alexander III, agreed to what his father had begun, but from the first he took a more jaundiced view of Bismarck and the Germans, in part no doubt because of the influence of his Danish wife, who had neither forgotten nor forgiven Bismarck for Prussia's 1864 war against Denmark. But Alexander III also had a weakness for Pan-Slavism and its imperial ambitions in Bulgaria and at the straits, ambitions that he believed Austria-Hungary, with German support, would attempt to thwart. Konstantin Pobedonostsev, the influential procurator of the Holy Synod—administrative head of the Russian Orthodox Church—only encouraged the headstrong tsar in his prejudices and goals.

One who attempted to rein in the tsar was Nikolai Karlovich Giers, the Russian foreign minister whom Kennan ranked second only to Bismarck among European diplomats of the second half of the nineteenth century. Of Swedish origin but thoroughly Russianized, Giers, Kennan wrote, belonged to that faction in Russian public life that was content with Russia's international position and that therefore wished to act in a restrained manner so as to preserve peace with Germany and Austria-Hungary. Giers and other members of this faction tended, according to Kennan, "to be either people of conservative disposition or people of a certain international sophistication, or both."[55]

Giers found himself up against formidable odds, not so much in his dealings with Bismarck and other foreign leaders, but in those with the tsar and influential Russian nationalists such as the prominent newspaper editor Mikhail Katkov. While the foreign minister believed it to be in Russia's national interest to preserve the Dreikaiserbund, Katkov urged its abandonment. Meanwhile, Alexander III's hostile attitude toward Austria-Hungary and to a lesser extent Germany, was made more dangerous by events in Bulgaria.

In 1879, his father had chosen his favorite nephew, Alexander von Battenberg of the house of Hesse-Darmstadt, as prince of Bulgaria. For reasons never fully made clear, Alexander III conceived a hatred for the young prince that nothing could abate. Even though the Russians had, since the Congress of Berlin, desired the unification of Bulgaria and Eastern Rumelia (by their efforts), the tsar was beside himself when he received news that Battenberg, whose hand had been forced by a nationalist insurrection in Eastern Rumelia, had taken the lead in a successful movement for unification.

The Pan-Slavs helped to persuade the incensed tsar that the Austrians—and probably the Germans—had been in some way responsible for Battenberg's actions and that the Dreikaiserbund stood in the way of Russia's ability to act freely in its own interest. The military, led by Chief of the General Staff Nikolai Obruchev (whose brother was a revolutionary), made the argument that Russia's problems could be solved only by war with Austria-Hungary; while opposing any renewal of the Dreikaiserbund, the officer corps favored a military alliance with France.

In France, meanwhile, fanatical nationalists such as the poet Paul Déroulède and editor Juliette Adam lobbied for a French-Russian accord. The government chose to proceed with caution; it preferred, Kennan maintained, to wait for the Russians to come to them. Nevertheless, revenge and the recovery of Alsace and Lorraine remained goals shared by all Frenchmen—witness the popular enthusiasm for General Georges Boulanger, the longed-for "Liberator of Alsace-Lorraine," who, with power seemingly within his grasp, lost his nerve and, in 1891, shot himself on the grave of his mistress.

Alexander III's growing interest in France had nothing to do with Alsace and Lorraine and everything to do with his Balkan ambitions. He knew that before he could wage war against Austria-Hungary he would have to be sure that Germany would be kept busy fighting France. This argued caution. But his inability to control events in Bulgaria stuck in his craw. Even when Battenberg gave up trying to restore himself to the tsar's good graces and abdicated, Alexander III was unappeased. Before stepping down, the prince had appointed a three-man regency unfriendly to Russia; charged with responsibility for choosing a new prince, it turned to Prince Ferdinand of Saxe-Coburg-Gotha. The very fact that the young man had been selected by the regency was enough to infuriate the tsar; it had become for him, Giers told the Austrians, a question of "amour-propre."[56] Because he continued to suspect Austro-Hungarian and German skullduggery, it was only with the greatest effort that Giers was able to convince him to agree to a three-year extension of the Dreikaiserbund.

By 1887, however, it had become clear to Giers that the tsar would not agree to another extension. The worn-out foreign minister did manage, however, to obtain Alexander III's grudging agreement to a secret "Reinsurance Treaty" with Germany alone. The two powers promised to observe neutrality should either become involved in war with a third power—not to apply in the event that Germany attacked France or Russia attacked Austria-Hungary. Germany declared itself neutral with respect to any Russian action at the straits and recognized Russia's preponderant influence in Bulgaria. The treaty was, on Bismarck's part, a stroke of genius. Not only did he secure Germany against the danger of a Franco-Russian alliance, but he checkmated Russia and Austria-Hungary. Germany would stand by the party attacked; thereby he put a premium on peace.

Despite the tsar's suspicions, Bismarck never thought of going to war with Russia. Kennan had no difficulty in understanding the Iron Chancellor's reasoning: "What would be Germany's objectives in such a war? The conquest of new territory? But the

Germans wanted no Russian territory. The destruction of the Russian armed forces? But a total destruction of them was not possible. . . . For what, then, would the Germans be fighting? For what would they be prepared to settle? It was always easier to start a war, he [Bismarck] pointed out, than to end one."[57]

Giers was equally reasonable and responsible, a man recognized for "his long and faithful adherence to the principles of restraint and conciliation in his dealings with the representatives of the other Powers."[58] If only the tsar had possessed the same virtues! Blind to problems at home—very much including the revolutionary movement—he inclined his ear to Pan-Slavs and military leaders who saw in an alliance with France an opportunity to secure control of the Balkans and the straits. And when in March 1888 Kaiser Wilhelm I died (to be followed to the grave three months later by his son and successor, Friedrich III) and Wilhelm II ascended to the German throne, the tsar found a new reason for his anti-German feeling: he could not abide his brash and blustering relative.

The new kaiser, believing that his family tie to Alexander III was a sufficient guarantee of good relations with Russia, and in any case receptive to the military's anti-Russian views, elected not to renew the Reinsurance Treaty when it expired in 1890. At the same time, he decided, in his wisdom, that Germany could do without the continued services of the great chancellor. Kennan summed up his personality nicely. "In contrast to both the old Kaiser [i.e., Wilhelm I] and Bismarck, who were in many respects eighteenth-century personalities, he was very much a product of the late nineteenth century, with all its inner uncertainties and extravagant pretensions."[59]

Kennan had titled this first of a projected three-volume work *The Decline of Bismarck's European Order* (1979). That decline paved the way for the Franco-Russian alliance that was the subject of the second (and as it turned out, final) volume in the series: *The Fateful Alliance: France, Russia, and the Coming of the First*

*World War* (1984). Published—by a commercial press—in the year that he turned eighty, the book was the product of archival research that would have challenged far younger scholars. Kennan had worked in the Archives des affairs étrangères at the Quai d'Orsay in Paris; the Haus-, Hof-, und Staatsarchiv in Vienna; the Arkhiv Vneshnei Politiki in Moscow; the Public Record Office in London; and the Overhofmarskallatetsarkiv and foreign-office archives in Copenhagen.

By 1890, as readers of the preceding volume knew, the die had been cast, but Kennan provided a detailed account of the meetings that took place between General-Adjutant Obruchev and French General Raoul le Mouton de Boisdeffre, for both of whom the creation of the alliance had become a life's work. On August 18, 1892, the two men signed a military convention that constituted the basis for the Franco-Russian alliance, formally approved (with Giers's consent, but regret) by Alexander III on December 17, 1893, and by the French government on January 4, 1894. It stipulated that if France were to be attacked by Germany, or by Italy supported by Germany, Russia would attack Germany. If Russia were to be attacked by Germany, or by Austria-Hungary supported by Germany, France would attack Germany. In the event that the Triple Alliance (concluded in 1882) or one of its signatories (i.e., Germany, Austria-Hungary, or Italy) should mobilize, France and Russia would immediately do the same.

There was, however, a contradiction between the first and second articles. In the second, France bound herself to mobilize even if Austria-Hungary alone mobilized; in the first, only if Germany mobilized, or Austria-Hungary supported by Germany. Russia's obligations were similarly contradictory. Both countries seem to have reasoned that in a pinch, they could say that they could not be expected to mobilize in cases in which they were not expected to fight—and both promised to keep their agreement secret.

Kennan had told the story of the alliance with his usual skill and eloquence, but he was equally interested in the lessons to be learned from its telling. "Without a generation of civilized people to study history, to preserve its records, to absorb its lessons and relate them to their own problems," he told an audience in 1984, the year that *The Fateful Alliance* appeared, "history, too, would lose its meaning."[60] One of the alliance's lessons, according to Kennan, was that it is dangerous to allow amateurs—propagandists and meddlers—to wield influence in foreign affairs equal to or greater than that of professional diplomats; whatever Katkov's virtues as an editor, for example, he lacked Giers's training and experience—and hence his measured good sense.

Another lesson was that it is always dangerous to view relations between states strictly in military terms. The alliance, Kennan rightly observed, "was a purely military document. Nothing was said in it about the political objectives for which one might be fighting."[61] Here he was drawing on the wisdom of Clausewitz, who famously asserted that "war is nothing but the continuation of politics with the admixture of other means." The German believed that war, to be justified, had to serve realistic political goals. "The political object is the goal," he wrote, "war is the means of reaching it, and means can never be considered in isolation from their purposes."[62]

To formulate objectives would be—as it was in the dynastic wars of the eighteenth century—to set limits, but the Great War, Kennan had come to believe, was limitless in its aims. "Victory was to be either total or overwhelmingly decisive; and it was, in this sense, regarded as an objective in itself." Cut loose from rational, limited, political objectives, modern wars unleashed nationalist frenzies that tended "to obliterate, in minds of both statesmen and popular masses, all consciousness of that essential community of fate that links, in reality, all great nations of the modern world and renders the destruction of any one of them the ultimate destruction, too, of the country that destroyed it."[63] In a nuclear age, that destruction would truly be total.

◆◆◆

In a speech he delivered in Germany on October 1, 1980, Kennan made the purpose of his historical work perfectly clear:

> If we, the scholars, with our patient and unsensational labors, can help the statesmen to understand . . . not only the dangers we face and the responsibility they bear for overcoming these dangers but also the constructive and hopeful possibilities that lie there to be opened up by wiser, more restrained, and more realistic policies . . . we will be richly repaid for our dedication and our persistence; for we will then have the satisfaction of knowing that scholarship, the highest work of the mind, has served, as it should, the highest interests of civilization.[64]

As Kennan argued repeatedly, the greatest danger facing civilization was nuclear war. It may seem, in retrospect, that he exaggerated that danger. Despite his efforts, President Truman issued a directive, in January 1950, to continue work on the hydrogen (H) bomb and all other forms of nuclear weapons. Nuclear arsenals grew, yet neither the United States nor the Soviet Union ever unleashed their weapons of mass destruction. Nevertheless, we know that the Cuban missile crisis brought the world to the brink of disaster—and even after that bullet was dodged, there were American hawks who spoke with conviction of "winning" a nuclear war. The danger that so troubled Kennan was a real one.

To Kennan, talk of winning a nuclear war was as irrational as it was immoral. Even without nuclear weapons, a Third

World War would, in his view, be the final catastrophe. "What would be left," he told an audience in 1982, "would be not worth survival."[65] A nuclear holocaust would destroy all hope of human survival, a realistic conclusion that seemed to escape many American leaders, including Walt Rostow, who in 1961 assumed the directorship of the Policy Planning Staff. When Rostow announced it as his view that a nuclear war could be won, Kennan exploded in anger. He would rather see his children dead, he told his successor, than have them experience such a war.

Shortly after the Soviets detonated a "nuclear device" in 1949, Kennan, who was at the end of his tenure as director of the Policy Planning Staff, prepared a personal "memorandum" for Secretary of State Acheson; looking back over his long government career, he judged that paper to have been his most important. In it he urged Acheson not to support the development of the "Super"—a thermonuclear (fusion) bomb—without at least first seeking an arms-control agreement with the Soviet Union. In any event, however, he argued that it was important that the government decide whether or not nuclear weapons were to constitute an integral component of U.S. military strength. If they were not to be so regarded—as Kennan urged—they should, in sensible numbers, be retained only for purposes of deterrence and retaliation.

With such a deterrent and a strengthening of conventional arms, the U.S. could and should renounce any first use of nuclear weapons and work for some kind of international control. The latter recommendation was less realistic than the former, but neither convinced Acheson or anyone else in the government—except Robert Oppenheimer, who, in addition to his duties at the Institute for Advanced Study, was then acting as chairman of the General Advisory Committee to the Atomic Energy Commission (AEC).

"No man," Oppenheimer's most recent biographers have written, "had stimulated Kennan's thinking about the myriad dangers of the nuclear age more than Oppenheimer."[66] That is true, not least because Oppenheimer possessed as great a knowledge of nuclear weapons as any man alive. He had been scientific director of the Manhattan Project and was often referred to as the "father" of the atomic bomb. The destruction of Hiroshima and Nagasaki had, however, awakened in him a dread of all-out nuclear war, and, like Kennan, he voiced strong opposition to the development of the H-bomb.

In the second volume of his memoirs, Kennan penned an affectionate portrait of Oppenheimer, of whose greatness he entertained no doubt. Out of both conviction and loyalty, he defended his friend against the charges that led, in 1954, to the revocation of his security clearance. "I can conceive of no motive" for the charge of unreliability, Kennan wrote, "other than personal vindictiveness and shameless, heartless political expediency."[67] Although he did not name names, he was thinking of William L. Borden, former executive director of the Joint Committee on Atomic Energy; Lewis Strauss, chairman of the AEC; and Edward Teller, the Hungarian-born "father" of the H-bomb.

It was Borden who in a letter to J. Edgar Hoover charged that Oppenheimer was (probably) spying for the Soviets and thus set in motion the ultimately successful effort to discredit him. The vindictive Strauss was only too quick to ask Hoover for a summary of Oppenheimer's FBI file; he had been looking for an opportunity to strike back at the physicist ever since the day in May 1949 when, at a congressional committee hearing, Oppenheimer had humiliated him in a debate over the wisdom of shipping iron isotopes abroad. Strauss stated his opposition to doing so because he feared that the isotopes might be put to military use, whereupon Oppenheimer mocked him by pointing out that almost anything could be used for military purposes and by conceding, sarcastically, that isotopes did present a greater danger in that regard than vitamins.

Teller, who had worked with Oppenheimer at Los Alamos, claimed in his memoirs that he had testified reluctantly at the closed hearing (April 12–May 6, 1954) that Oppenheimer had requested—the alternative before him was resignation—in the hope of clearing his name. That may be so, but his testimony was damaging. He did not, he told the inquisitors, believe that his colleague was disloyal, but Teller did feel that he would "like to see the vital interests of this country in hands which I understand better, and therefore trust more."[68]

Teller's personal reputation suffered irreparable damage as a result of his appearance at the hearing. He later conceded that readers of his testimony could be forgiven for concluding that it was Oppenheimer's lack of enthusiasm for the thermonuclear project that made him uneasy, but he insisted that it was instead the so-called "Chevalier affair." Sometime during the winter of 1942–43, Oppenheimer and his wife, who were then preparing to leave the University of California at Berkeley, invited Haakon Chevalier, a professor of French literature, and his wife for dinner. Both men were political leftists and, according to an unpublished memoir by the late Gordon Griffiths, who was then working for the Communist Party, both had been members of a faculty communist cell.

Oppenheimer always denied that he had been a party member, but he was probably lying. We know that he made monthly contributions to the party until 1942. By the time of the dinner, he may well have been having second thoughts about communism, but we also know from Soviet intelligence archives that he did give the Soviets "cooperation in access to research" from 1942 to 1944.[69]

Chevalier was not having any difficulty retaining his faith. Finding Oppenheimer alone in the kitchen, he reported that George Eltenton, a British-born chemical engineer in the employ of the Shell Oil Company, had asked that he sound Oppenheimer out with respect to a possible willingness to pass information to a Soviet diplomat—in reality an intelligence agent—concerning his work at Berkeley's Radiation Laboratory (Rad Lab). In no uncertain terms, Oppenheimer told Chevalier that to pass the Soviets information of that nature would be an act of treason.

Was Oppenheimer suffering from a guilty conscience? He never reported this attempted recruitment, probably because he feared that to do so would trigger a full investigation, or at least create difficulties for Chevalier and Eltenton. But in the event, silence merely delayed matters. His past and his associations with known Communist Party members, including his wife, his brother Frank, and his lover Jean Tatlock, continued to attract the attention of counterintelligence. Oppenheimer was quite aware of this, and in late August 1943, he told the army security officer at Rad Lab that Eltenton, who had once lived in the USSR, should be watched. The following day, Colonel Boris Pash, Chief of Counter-Intelligence on the West Coast, had Oppenheimer brought in for interrogation. Unbeknownst to Oppenheimer, it was recorded.

Pash drew Oppenheimer into a discussion of those who might be interested in the work at Rad Lab, and before he knew it he was saying that he was aware of three Soviet-initiated approaches to other scientists with whom he worked, though he refused to name them. He again gave it as his view that it would be wise to keep an eye on Eltenton and said that someone acting for the Shell engineer—whom he refused to identify—had made the approaches, though only by way of providing information or of working to aid the Soviets, allies of the United States, in their life-or-death struggle against Nazi Germany. In Oppenheimer's (probably sincere) view, it was all rather innocent.

Pash and General Leslie R. Groves, military chief of the Manhattan Project, thought otherwise. In December 1943, Groves ordered Oppenheimer to identify Eltenton's intermediary. Oppenheimer promptly named Chevalier, adding that his brother Frank was one of the three individuals approached. Frank Oppenheimer denied this.

That was not the end of it. In June 1946, the FBI questioned both Eltenton and Chevalier about their contact with Oppenheimer in 1943. Both men supported Oppenheimer's claim that he angrily rejected any idea of "sharing" scientific secrets with the Soviet Union, but both denied having approached anyone else. Three months later, it was Oppenheimer's turn, and he repeated what he had told Pash concerning his kitchen conversation with Chevalier. Or almost. When pressed about the alleged three approaches to other scientists, he confessed that he had "concocted" the story in order to shield Chevalier. In other words, he had lied to Pash. When asked why at his 1954 hearing, he said only: "Because I was an idiot."[70]

What ought one to make of all this? That Oppenheimer performed valuable services for his country is a matter of record. So is the fact that he was an active member of the Congress for Cultural Freedom. Those who stripped him of his clearance did not know about his wartime "cooperation" with the Soviets, whatever that may have meant; they did know, however, that Oppenheimer had been a Soviet sympathizer and that he had not always told the truth—which did not exactly inspire confidence. Kennan seemed to recognize this even as he acted as a character witness for his friend. It was a fact, he told those sitting in judgment of Oppenheimer, "that when gifted individuals come to a maturity of judgment which makes them valuable public servants, you are apt to find that the road by which they have approached that has not been as regular as the road by which other people have approached it. It may have zigzags in it of various sorts."[71]

In a piece he wrote for the *New York Review of Books* in 1994, Kennan again gave it as his "deepest conviction" that his late friend could not have betrayed his country. Never, he recalled, had Oppenheimer ever expressed to him so much as the faint-est admiration or sympathy for the Soviet regime. But Kennan conceded that Oppenheimer had been persuaded by physicist Niels Bohr that it would have been wise to have included Soviet scientists in the project to develop the atom bomb. And he could not and did not deny that his belief in his friend's innocence was a matter of general judgment concerning his character—"it was not in his nature"—and not of any personal knowledge of his wartime activities.[72]

Kennan viewed Oppenheimer's ordeal as but one, though a particularly egregious, example of an anticommunism that had developed into a semireligious cult. Because of his own impec-cable anticommunist credentials and his refusal to be intimidat-ed, he did not hesitate to speak loudly and clearly against what he regarded as a national spirit of fanaticism and vindictiveness. Nevertheless, he discovered that he was able to do little to save the career and reputation of John Paton Davies Jr., who had served under him in Moscow and on the Policy Planning Staff; an "old China hand," Davies became the target of a witch-hunt because of his critical view of the Chinese Nationalist govern-ment and his belief that the communists would emerge victori-ous in China's civil war.

In the atmosphere of McCarthyism, these were unforgivable sins, and, after watching him testify before various congression-al committees, John Foster Dulles dismissed Davies from the foreign service "for lack of judgment, discretion and reliability." Kennan was appalled by the treatment Davies received and by the State Department's failure to come to his defense. The case witnessed to an exaggerated fear of communist subversion, the reality of which Kennan never denied. Such an overrating of an external (Soviet) threat, he believed, represented, "in bodies of people just as in individuals, a failure of the critical faculty when applied to oneself—a failure of self-knowledge."[73]

◆◆◆

On November 22, 1977, Kennan delivered a speech before a Council on Foreign Relations session in Washington, D.C. It had been thirty years since the publication of his "X" article and he wished to call his listeners' attention to the fact that much had changed in Soviet Russia. In 1947, the country had been at the mercy of a despot as ruthless as any the modern world had ever witnessed. Stalin maintained monopolistic control over communist movements worldwide—a control that meant that a communist success anywhere was equivalent to a Soviet conquest. Hence the need for a policy of containment.

By 1977, however, the Soviet Union had evolved from a totalitarian to an authoritarian state. The era of terror was no more, and Soviet leaders, all of whom were advanced in age, had no desire for rash adventures. Kennan described Leonid Brezhnev as a "conservative man," a man "confidently regarded by all who know him as a man of peace." That being the case, he could not understand why hard-liners on the American right continued to view Soviet-American relations as they had during the height of the Cold War—they "sometimes seem, in fact, unaware that Stalin is dead."[74]

Some of those people, Kennan observed, had become so aroused over "human rights" and Jewish emigration that they sought not an accommodation with the Soviet Union but a fundamental change in the Soviet system. Others—and Kennan viewed them as the greater danger to peace—looked upon Soviet-American competition exclusively in military terms and indulged in fantastic speculation concerning the numbers and destructive potentialities of various weapons, including nuclear weapons. Those weapons made it imperative that those responsible for the conduct of American foreign policy not be misled by a view of Soviet Russia that was profoundly anachronistic.

Kennan's speech was published in the March 1978 issue of *Encounter,* the splendid magazine that had been launched with funds secretly provided by the CIA. In the April issue of the same magazine, Richard Pipes, a professor of Russian history at Harvard and a personal friend, published a scathing attack on Kennan's views. Of Polish-Jewish origin, Pipes was a leading Russophobe and hard-line anticommunist. He insisted that there had been no transformations in the basic institutions of Soviet state and society and that it was therefore "inappropriate to speak of 'changes' of any magnitude having occurred in the Soviet Union since 1953."[75]

Pipes saw nothing "rightist" about a concern with an effective military defense and took strong exception to Kennan's oft-repeated view that there could be no victor in a nuclear war–and hence that the whole issue of nuclear superiority was meaningless. He appealed to the contrary opinions of Paul Nitze, a successor to Kennan at the Policy Planning Staff who did indeed have very different ideas, and to the views of Edward Luttwak, a prominent policy analyst. "I myself," he added, "have called attention to the war-fighting and war-winning elements in Soviet nuclear doctrine."[76] For Kennan's characterization of Brezhnev as a man of peace, Pipes had nothing but contempt. What, he asked rhetorically, about the invasion of Czechoslovakia, the threats to China and Romania, the conspiracies against Israel, the assistance to North Vietnam, the subversive activities in Africa?

In the next issue of *Encounter,* Kennan published an uncharacteristically biting reply to Pipes and, to a lesser degree, other critics. He pronounced himself unimpressed by Pipes's argument concerning the stability of Soviet institutions. Institutions, as Tocqueville had pointed out, were merely frameworks; what mattered most was *les manières.* "American institutions, too, have remained extraordinarily stable over many decades; yet we are a quite different society than we were some time ago."[77] Anyone

GEORGE KENNAN: A WRITING LIFE

unable to discern any significant difference between the Russia of 1953 and of 1977 could not be taken seriously.

Kennan was particularly incensed by Pipes's insinuation that he lacked an appreciation of the dark side of Soviet rule. "I did not think," he wrote, "that I needed any instruction on this subject. . . . I have stated my views on these matters, I thought reasonably explicitly, on a number of occasions; and I see no reason for the ritualistic incantation of them at frequent intervals just to meet the fashion of the times."[78]

Kennan went on to state forcefully and unapologetically that he and his critics did have a serious disagreement concerning nuclear weapons. "I must totally reject the suggestion," he wrote, "that any war fought with these great arsenals, or with ones even a tenth their size, could be 'winnable'—that it could be, in fact, anything less than a catastrophe of apocalyptic dimensions for all concerned, and millions not concerned."[79] With respect to Brezhnev and Soviet aggression in Czechoslovakia, the Near East, and Africa, Kennan explained, rather impatiently, that he referred to the Soviet leader's obvious disinclination to become involved in a major war with Western powers. Never, he reminded his critics, had the Soviet Union attacked a *major* adversary.

That this debate should have taken place in the pages of *Encounter* was most fitting. Founded in 1953 by Irving Kristol and Stephen Spender, the magazine was strongly anticommunist and moderately social democratic in outlook. Many of its contributors, including Arthur Koestler, were former communists of the "God that failed" school. Spender had been one of the contributors to the famous symposium of that title, and Kristol was a former Trotskyite. Having awakened from their dogmatic slumber, they, like Pipes, saw little difference between Stalin and Nikita Khrushchev, or Stalin and Brezhnev.

When during the 1960s a "New Left" burst onto the scene, many of those who had written for *Encounter* were appalled. Liberals and social democrats, the Americans among them were Democrats who admired FDR, Truman, and Kennedy. They had no use for Senator George McGovern, the Democrats' 1972 presidential nominee; they regarded him and President Jimmy Carter as soft on communism. They did admire Senator Henry "Scoop" Jackson, Democrat of Washington, a hard-liner with respect to the Soviet Union and cosponsor of the Jackson-Vanik amendment to the 1974 Trade Reform Act. That amendment, which Kennan thought both pointless and unnecessarily offensive, denied normal trade relations to countries that restricted freedom of emigration. It was aimed at the Soviet Union, which was then attempting, with limited success, to restrict Jewish emigration.

Jackson was, however, an exception. Anticommunist liberals and social democrats began to gravitate toward the Republican Party, thus earning for themselves the (originally pejorative) name of "neoconservatives." As the so-called "godfather" of the neoconservatives, Irving Kristol described the historical task of this new conservatism to be "to convert the Republican party, and American conservatism in general, against their respective wills, into a new kind of conservative politics suitable to governing a modern democracy."[80] With respect to foreign policy, neoconservatives adopted a hard line in relations with the Soviet Union and believed it to be America's responsibility to spread democracy around the world; theirs was, then, a neo-Wilsonianism.

Neoconservatives cheered the electoral victory of Ronald Reagan in 1980. Kennan did not. He believed the new president and the administration he led to be too belligerent, too persuaded that the Soviet leaders behaved properly only when confronted by superior military force, especially nuclear. By 1982, he had all but given up hope that the administration would be able to conduct serious and responsible negotiations with the USSR. "There are strong signs," he told an audience at Union Theological Seminary, "that the Soviet leaders have given up on the Reagan administration, in the sense that they have concluded they have nothing to expect at its hands except a total, blind, and almost deadly hostility, and that not much is to be gained by trying to talk with it."[81] When, in a speech of March 8, 1983, before the National Association of Evangelicals, the president described the Soviet Union as an "evil empire," Kennan was even more certain that Soviet-American relations would continue to worsen and that the nuclear danger would only increase.

Kennan was wrong about President Reagan, who, we now know, shared his abhorrence of nuclear weapons. "For the eight years I was president," Reagan wrote in his memoirs, "I never let my dream of a nuclear-free world fade from my mind."[82] He was telling the truth. Many, like Kennan, failed to recognize that truth because the president had an unconventional way of pursuing his goal of abolishing all nuclear weapons. Believing as he did that a nuclear war could not be "won" and that Mutual Assured Destruction (MAD) was both immoral and unacceptably risky, he resolved to force negotiations in a new and more promising direction.

That would not be easy, Reagan knew, for during his first term he had to deal with a sclerotic Brezhnev, a terminally ill Yuri Andropov, and a geriatric Konstantin Chernenko. Like Kennan he believed that those Soviet leaders were confronted with serious problems at home, especially with respect to the Soviet economy. He reasoned that he could, by forcing them to engage in all-out competition, particularly in the sphere of military spending, bring them to recognize that it was in their interest to agree to substantive nuclear-arms reductions.

After the March 30, 1981, attempt on his life, Reagan became even more determined to rid the world of nuclear weapons. "Perhaps having come so close to death," he wrote in his memoirs, "made me feel I should do whatever I could in the years God had given me to reduce the threat of nuclear war."[83] Few members of his administration understood the depth of his commitment, and fewer still sympathized with it. Not surprisingly, Pipes, whom national security advisor Richard Allen had chosen to be his director of Soviet and Eastern European affairs, was dismayed by Reagan's strong antinuclear views.

Pipes and other administration officials were even more disconcerted when, late in 1982, Reagan ordered the Joint Chiefs of Staff to explore the possibility of a missile defense system. "What," he asked them, "if we began to move away from our total reliance on offense to deter a nuclear attack and moved toward a relatively greater reliance on defense?"[84] On March 23, 1983, he announced his Strategic Defense Initiative (SDI)—always referred to by a hostile press as "Star Wars" in order to suggest that the president was delusional. The concept was simple; instead of an ever-escalating arms race dedicated to offense, the U.S. would focus upon defense. If a system could be devised to intercept and destroy ballistic missiles, nuclear weapons would lose much of their value and their elimination would become more rational.

The press and many in the administration scoffed at the president's idea—it was, they insisted, too expensive, if not implausible. Kennan thought the plan unhelpful with respect to negotiations with the Soviets. But Andropov panicked when told of SDI—which he and his advisors seemed to think technologically possible. "Reagan is unpredictable," he warned. "You should expect anything from him."[85] He was not mollified by the president's offer, sincerely made, to share a successful SDI once agreement had been reached to eliminate nuclear weapons. Nor did the former KGB chief sleep any better at night after receiving a personal communication from the president in July: "Can we as leaders of our two nations allow the people we represent + their children to look toward a future in which they must live under the threat of these destructive weapons? What a blessing [the elimination of nuclear weapons] would be for the people we both represent."[86]

In his second inaugural address, delivered on January 21, 1985, Reagan reiterated his determination to rid the world of nuclear weapons. Whether or not Chernenko, who had succeeded Andropov on February 13, 1984, was even well enough to respond is unclear; he died on March 10, 1985. The new Soviet leader, Mikhail Gorbachev, was a man of very different stamp, though that was not immediately obvious. He too took a dim view of SDI and repeatedly tried to force Reagan to shelve the plan. Secretary of State George Shultz, national security advisor Robert McFarlane, and arms-control "czar" Paul Nitze concluded that SDI could at least be useful as a bargaining chip in negotiations with the Soviets.

The three men seemed unable to understand that Reagan would never trade SDI away—he truly believed in it as the best hope for eliminating nuclear weapons. And although he could not persuade Gorbachev of his good intentions when the two men met in Geneva in November 1985, he nevertheless came away encouraged. Unlike some of his advisors, he recognized in the fifty-four-year-old Gorbachev a different type of Soviet leader, one with whom he might achieve meaningful breakthroughs toward a safer and more peaceful world. That possibility became even more real as a result of the disastrous explosion at the Chernobyl nuclear power plant on April 26, 1986. "Chernobyl," Gorbachev wrote in his memoirs, "made me and my colleagues rethink a great many things."[87]

The following October, Reagan and Gorbachev met again, this time in Reykjavik, Iceland. Both men proposed substantial cuts in existing weaponry, but the Soviet leader persisted in his demand that SDI be confined to laboratory testing, even when the president repeated his earlier offer to share the technology. In a rare display of public anger, Reagan ended the summit. Nevertheless, the recognition that Gorbachev shared his de-

George Kennan in 1925

*Photograph courtesy of Princeton University Library*

Taking the oath as Ambassador to the USSR in 1952
with Mrs. Kennan and his daughter, Grace

*Photograph courtesy of Princeton University Library*

Playing the guitar

Belgrade,
Yugoslavia, 1962

*Photograph courtesy of*
*Princeton University Library*

With President Tito

Yugoslavia, 1962

*Photograph courtesy of*
*Princeton University Library*

In Kristiansand, Norway,
1966

*Photograph courtesy of Princeton University Library*

146 Hodge Road,
The Kennan Residence in Princeton

*Photograph by Carol Congdon*

Fuld Hall
Institute for Advanced Study

*Photograph by Carol Congdon*

Kennan's words engraved near the Institute Woods.

"True scholars often work in loneliness, compelled to find reward in the awareness
that they have made valuable, even beautiful, contributions to the cumulative structure of human knowledge, whether anyone knows it at the time or not."

*Photograph by Carol Congdon*

# The Institute Woods

*Photographs by Carol Congdon*

Final place of rest,
the Princeton Cemetery

*Photograph by Carol Congdon*

sire to abolish nuclear weapons was important to him. When they met a third time, in Washington in December 1987, they did agree to dismantle intermediate-range nuclear missiles in Europe. Kennan was pleased, though, rather uncharitably, he gave most of the credit to Gorbachev. "Hundreds of millions of people the world over," he wrote, "electrified by Gorbachev's striking appearance at the Washington summit, have been moved to a new level of hope for real progress, at long last, in the overcoming of the nuclear nightmare."[88]

Thanks to both men there had been progress by January 20, 1989, the day Reagan's second term came to an end. Moreover, the Cold War itself was nearing a conclusion. In the same year, the Eastern European satellites, beginning with Poland and Hungary, fell like dominos, and with remarkably little violence. Only in Romania was there bloodshed, with the removal by firing squad of the unhinged dictator, Nicolai Ceausescu. In the same month—December—that Ceausescu met his end, Gorbachev and the new president, George Bush, met at Malta. Bush admitted that the United States had been surprised and shaken by the fast-moving events in Eastern Europe.

Gorbachev received praise, even adulation, for the role he had played in liberating the peoples of Eastern Europe—but not in the Soviet Union, where his hard-line policy toward Lithuania led to confusion and where chaos threatened. On August 18, 1991, a group of inept plotters placed the beleaguered leader under house arrest in the Crimea and attempted to stage a coup. It failed miserably, thanks in part to the public stand taken by Boris Yeltsin, who had been elected president of Russia in June. Yeltsin, who disliked Gorbachev, used his growing popularity to replace his rival as the leader who commanded the most authority. He used that authority to abolish the Communist Party of the Soviet Union and to organize, with Ukraine and Byelorussia, a "Commonwealth of Independent States." Gorbachev's protests were to no avail and, on Christmas Day 1991, he handed over to Yeltsin the nuclear codes and signed a decree that ended the seventy-four-year existence of the USSR.

The death of the USSR took the so-called Sovietologists completely by surprise. As late as 1983, eight of them had contributed learned essays to a book titled *After Brezhnev*. The editor, Robert Byrnes, informed readers that it was his and his colleagues' considered opinion "that there is no likelihood whatsoever that the Soviet Union will become a political democracy or that it will collapse in the foreseeable future."[89] A year later, John Kenneth Galbraith, an admirer of "planned" economies, gave his assurance that the "Soviet system has made great economic progress in recent years."[90] One could easily cite other examples of the same kind of certainty.

Among the few who possessed a clearer vision, two are worth mentioning. In 1969, Russian dissident Andrei Amalrik questioned whether the Soviet Union would survive until 1984, the year made famous by George Orwell's novel of a perfected totalitarianism. Even more striking, perhaps, was *Times* of London columnist Bernard Levin's piece of August 1977. He predicted that someone would emerge from within the CPSU ruling class who would preside over the dissolution of the USSR—one of those who were then obeying orders and performing their duties. "They do not conspire, they are not in touch with Western intelligence agencies, they commit no sabotage," but they had admitted to themselves bitter truths about their country.

Levin went on to describe how the collapse would occur. "There will be no gunfire in the streets, no barricades, no general strikes, no hanging of oppressors from lamp-posts, no sacking and burning of government offices, no seizure of radio-stations or mass defections among the military." As for when these events would unfold—"let us suppose, for neatness' sake, on July 14, 1989," the bicentennial of the storming of the Bastille.[91]

Kennan, we know, had foreseen the Soviet collapse as early as 1932, and in later years he had pointed out repeatedly that Soviet leaders were confronted with many serious problems. Yet insofar as he still believed a fall to be inevitable, he expected the decline to be gradual. Beyond the immediate causes of the sudden collapse lay, in his view, the regime's failure to deal effectively with the national question, as evidenced by the increasing demands, particularly in the Baltic region and Ukraine, for greater autonomy or even independence.[92]

Kennan was disturbed by the fact that after the breakup of the Soviet Union some in the West expressed fear of a new Russian expansionism. Such fear, he observed, was unwarranted. The Russians had during more than seventy years of communist rule suffered appalling injuries from which they had only begun to recover; they therefore wished to avoid, at almost any cost, new military involvements. For that and other reasons, Kennan saw no justification for expanding NATO to the east; whatever NATO leaders might say, such an enlargement could only be directed against Russia and place an unnecessary burden upon East-West relations. Nor did he display any enthusiasm for the NATO–U.S. bombing of Yugoslavia in the spring of 1999, although he did think that instability in the Balkans presented a problem for Europeans.

In the post–Cold War era, Kennan recommended what he had always recommended—that America pursue a more modest and restrained foreign policy, the better to attend to pressing problems at home. That was why he opposed the first President Bush's decision to send U.S. troops on a humanitarian mission—to make possible the delivery of food to starving people—to Somalia. On December 9, 1992, the day the first

American forces landed in the country, Kennan recorded his views in his diaries; they were subsequently published in the *New York Times.*

The dreadful situation in Somalia, he wrote, could only be put to rights by a ruthless governing power. America's intervention could offer no more than temporary relief to relatively small numbers of people, and at tremendous cost. "The dispatch of American armed forces to a seat of operations in a place far from our own shores, and this for what is actually a major police action in another country and in a situation where no defensible American interest is involved—this, obviously, is something that the Founding Fathers of this country never envisaged or would ever have approved."[93] He could not know then that in the following year President Clinton would make matters worse by ordering what turned out to be the bloody Battle of Mogadishu.

Unsympathetic as Kennan was to humanitarian interventions, he was not less unsympathetic to President George W. Bush's plans to wage war on Saddam Hussein's Iraq. Insofar as the Iraqi dictator posed a threat, Kennan declared in 2002, he did so to Israel, a country "quite capable of mounting a devastating retaliatory strike."[94] He added that one could never be certain in advance where a war would eventually lead. "I have seen no evidence that we have any realistic plans for dealing with the great state of confusion in Iraqian affairs which would presumably follow even after the successful elimination of the dictator."[95] Once again, one of his warnings went unheeded.

Kennan issued his warning as he approached the one hundredth anniversary of his birth. Knowing that little time remained to him, he felt a particular urgency to share with his countrymen whatever wisdom long years of experience and thoughtful reflection had vouchsafed him. America seemed to him to be determined to work against its own best interests by undertaking unwise interventions abroad while ignoring serious problems at home. What was to be done to save the country from itself?

Not wishing to succumb to despair, Kennan thought it important to offer concrete proposals that might lead in new national directions; for instance, he recommended the creation of a "Council of State" that would stand outside of politics and whose nine members would consider long-term problems and, after careful study and informed thought, make policy suggestions. Members of the council would be persons of high distinction and independent judgment—persons, one was left to conclude, like Kennan himself.

Kennan put forth his idea for a Council of State in a book that he wrote only after much hesitation: *Around the Cragged Hill: A Personal and Political Philosophy* (1993). He was, despite his public prominence, a very private person; moreover, he shared Burke's dislike of philosophic abstractions, which, he knew, a book of the kind he was planning would force upon him. Nevertheless, many admirers of his writing had insisted that he make explicit his personal and political philosophy, and he was moved by their interest and embarrassed by his reluctance to respond to their importunities. So he took the plunge.

In the opening chapter of his book, Kennan articulated a tragic sense of life that mirrored that of Freud, particularly the Freud of *Das Unbehagen in der Kultur* (translated into English as *Civilization and Its Discontents* [1930]). Man's animal origins, according to Kennan, set clear limits to his ability to civilize himself—and thus created in him a discontent for which he could identify no fully satisfactory reason and that accompanied him, to a greater or lesser extent, throughout his life. To act in a civilized manner, to elevate himself beyond animal instinct, was a constant struggle; he will always, he once told George Urban, feel a discomfort "at having to live in a civilized framework, and kick against it."[96] Nor, as Marxists and other utopians believed, could radical changes in economic and social arrangements put an end to the struggle, for "a measure of tragedy is built into the very existence of the human individual."[97]

What then, Kennan inquired, could be done about such a state of affairs? His answer was to have faith. Kennan's own religious faith is of the greatest importance for an understanding of his life and work; because he himself recognized this, he made, especially in his later years, profound and sustained efforts to gain spiritual self-knowledge. Never was there a time when he did not regard himself as a Christian, even when he was assailed by doubts concerning one or another aspect of orthodox teaching.

He was born, he once had occasion to remind his children, into a Presbyterian family, headed by a beloved father who grappled "fundamentally and agonizingly with the trials and dilemmas of faith" and who relied upon "the infinite mercy of God."[98] At St. John's Military Academy, a high-church Anglican institution, Kennan formed an attachment to the Episcopal Church, one strong enough to survive his years at Princeton, a Presbyterian university.

In common with many of his peers, he did not concern himself greatly with religious questions while at university or during his early years in the foreign service. Things began to change when he went to Russia. He felt nothing but disgust for Soviet efforts to substitute a pagan for a Christian sacramental life, and he became aware, for the first time, of his own dependence upon the latter. He sometimes attended the Russian Orthodox Church's Divine Liturgy, and on at least one occasion he visited an Orthodox monastery. He came to see in the Russian Church "the nearest thing (except perhaps the Armenian church) to early Christianity."[99] It left upon him a permanent mark, one that did not go unnoticed.

As he rose in the ranks of the foreign service, Kennan became increasingly aware that others looked to him for spiritual guidance. While serving as ambassador in Yugoslavia, he delivered carefully prepared sermons on a regular basis. On one occasion he spoke of science's inability to deal with the question of life after death; on another he defended the concept of original sin, though not Calvin's understanding of it, which he thought cruel and hopeless. On still another Sunday morning he denounced secularism and noted that to step outside the faith of one's fathers was to deny one's entire cultural heritage—a heritage of great beauty—and thus to forfeit the strength "that comes of being able to recognize one's self as a part of a continuity reaching beyond the present generation."[100]

It is worth noting that Kennan did not speak of political matters when conducting services. In his view, the duty of the church was not to issue political pronouncements but to teach man "to walk in God's ways, to extend to him the comfort of the sacraments, to support him in his moments of weakness, to console him in his failures, to teach him how to bear the heaviest of his sorrows, to maintain him in the strength of his belief."[101]

It was, one suspects, largely because he did not wish to abandon the faith of his fathers that, despite the attraction he felt for the Russian Orthodox Church, Kennan remained a Protestant. No doubt Anglicanism offered him a compromise between Protestantism and Orthodoxy; he often attended services at Princeton's Trinity Church, the more liberal of the city's two Episcopal parishes. Meanwhile, he continued to seek a fuller understanding of his own, highly personal, faith. In *Around the Cragged Hill,* he spoke of his belief in the universe's "Primary Cause"—what Gibbon had called the "Eternal Cause"—the "god" of the eighteenth-century deists. Having brought the universe into being and laid down the laws according to which it would operate, the Primary Cause promptly withdrew. It did not, in response to petitions from human beings, interfere in the workings of the laws it had established; in other words, non-natural events—miracles—did not occur.

Nor, in Kennan's view, did the Primary Cause concern itself with the travails of men; it remained supremely indifferent. Nevertheless, at some moment there emerged in man, but in no other animal, a self-consciousness of a rarefied kind—a soul, the existence of which was independent of the body. "Why," Kennan wondered, "to man and to none of the other animals? Here, if anywhere, one senses the intervention of a divine hand."[102] That hand could not have belonged to the Primary Cause, but only to the "Merciful Deity."

Unlike the Primary Cause, the Merciful Deity, or what on another occasion Kennan identified as the Holy Spirit, took an interest in and manifested a profound sympathy for man's trials and dilemmas. To be sure, He did not interrupt or alter the natural order, but He did stand with men in their struggles within that order. He was a loving companion, a pillar of strength in time of need. He and the Primary Cause formed no unity, were not one. Near the end of his life, however, Kennan changed his mind and began to identify the Holy Spirit with God the Father, thus linking two persons of the Trinity.

It was with respect to the third person of the Trinity, Christ, that Kennan was most ambivalent. "Even from the standpoint of the purely secular historian," he wrote in *Around the Cragged Hill,* "I would find the appearance of such a figure as Christ on this earth, at the place and the time of which history informs us, a most remarkable occurrence, bordering on the miraculous."[103] But was he the incarnate Son of God? Kennan seems never to have answered that question to his own satisfaction. He affirmed that Jesus truly *believed* that he was God's Son and that the spirit that spoke through him was of such profundity that it could only have been divine. But that was as far as he was prepared to go.

We recall that Kennan attributed to Helmuth von Moltke "a vision of Christianity broad, tolerant, and all-embracing, like that of Pasternak, in the range of its charity." His mention of the Russian writer—who, not so incidentally, admired Chekhov greatly—is instructive. Pasternak was the son of Leonid Pasternak, an impressionist and portrait painter, and Rosa Kaufman, a concert pianist. Jewish by birth, Pasternak *père* converted to Christianity, and Boris came to embrace a heterodox version of the same faith. "The atmosphere of [*Dr. Zhivago*]," Pasternak wrote to a friend, "is my Christianity."[104] And so it is. Kennan probably recognized Yuri Zhivago as the Christ figure he is; he obviously recognized in the physician-poet (who is also Pasternak himself) something of himself as a Christian.

"What makes Zhivago identical with Christ," Donald Davie perceptively observed, "is above all his capacity as an artist."[105] For Kennan, too, the holy was closely associated with the beautiful. One of the things he admired most about the Orthodox Church was "the great beauty of its ritual and its music";[106] such beauty seemed to him to witness to a spiritual reality. How else, he once asked rhetorically, do we account for the Requiem Mass of Mozart, a rather unpleasant young man whose personal experience of life could not account for the majesty of his music; his inspiration must have come from some other, and higher, source. By extension, Kennan believed, one could say the same of all the great artistic achievements of Western culture—in architecture, painting, sculpture, and poetry (in the broad sense of the German *Dichtung*).

But Kennan also praised the Orthodox Church "for its ready acceptance of the mysteries of faith."[107] There is a point at the end of the Orthodox funeral service, he commented late in life,

> when the casket has just been closed and the body is being
> carried out of the church, where the choir, in one of those

125

magnificent musical passages that are the glory of the Orthodox service, "sings" the immortal soul out of the now lifeless body and frees it for the pursuit of its passage to whatever awaits it in the afterlife. This image rests, in my mind, on a profound insight—an insight derived from the heart and not from the head. I accept it unquestionably.[108]

Near the end of his life, Kennan looked back upon his boyhood years in Milwaukee; every evening, he recalled, he knelt by his bed and recited the Lord's Prayer. The child that he then was never doubted that the words of that prayer were part of a great and solemn mystery, one not fully comprehensible but deserving of his respect and reverence. That experience remained for him a more enduring foundation for faith than all the questioning and reasoning of his adult years. As far as we know, it was with confidence in that foundation that he departed this world on March 17, 2005; a memorial service was held on April 6, at the National Cathedral (Episcopal) in Washington, D.C.

# 3

## Traditions of Thought

In the epilogue to *Around the Cragged Hill,* Kennan wrote, "I comfort myself with the thought that I can scarcely have been the first writer who learned what he thought only when he had looked at what he had written."[1] Of course, not all of his beliefs could be fitted into one volume. To learn what he thought, he would have had to read over the diaries, books, articles, letters, and speeches that had flowed from his pen over the course of a long life. He would then have been able to identify the traditions of thought to which he had made significant contributions.

The tradition of thought with which Kennan is most often identified is that of political realism. That tradition appears to most Americans to be rather foreign, incompatible with new-world enlightenment and morality. To them, diplomacy is morality as it applies to relations between states and to human conduct around the globe. The guiding principle of American foreign policy should therefore be to act in ways calculated to make the world a better place. Such a view presupposes that the moral principles embraced by Americans possess both perfect clarity and universal validity; their adoption by all men would lead inexorably to a world of peace and justice.

Realists take a different view. Those responsible for the conduct of foreign policy must, in their judgment, take the world as it is, not as it ought to be. They must recognize that the world is a dangerous place, because human nature, with its capacity for evil as well as good, remains constant, everywhere and at all times. In contrast to what most of his countrymen believed, for example, Kennan viewed man as a cracked vessel; as a result, the world in which he lives is, and will remain, fallen.

According to realists, the guiding principle in the conduct of foreign policy must be the national interest. That principle alone can give to policy a consistent and rational character. Far from being immoral, it prescribes prudent and hence moderate behavior. It rules out moral crusades that, however well-intentioned, inevitably produce more evil than good. For realists, in short, prudence is virtue as it is pursued in a political context in which the struggle for power is never wholly absent.

While conducting foreign policy, realists insist, a person acts under the authority of a standard of morality at some variance with that which governs his personal behavior. As an individual he may well choose to sacrifice his personal interest for some higher good—he may even obey the scriptural injunction to turn the other cheek. But insofar as he acts as the agent of others, of those whose welfare has been entrusted to him, he cannot, so to speak, turn a collective cheek. His duty is to defend their interests, not to sacrifice them to his own sense of right and wrong. That does not mean that he is free of moral responsibility; it means that the moral responsibility he has accepted as an agent is the well-being of those whom he serves.

The principle of political realism, or *raison d'état* as the French say, was first propounded and put into practice by Cardinal Richelieu, a prince of the church who was first minister of France from 1624 to 1642. So successful was the system that that principle dictated that it was adopted by virtually all European countries during the next three centuries. But only when the great Prussian/German chancellor, Otto von Bismarck, appeared on the scene did Richelieu find a truly worthy successor.

For Bismarck, *realpolitik* ruled out actions based upon personal prejudices—even the prejudices of those in authority. "I cannot," he observed, "reconcile personal sympathies and antipathies toward foreign powers with my sense of duty in foreign affairs; indeed I see in them the embryo of disloyalty toward the Sovereign and the country I serve. . . . Not even the King has the right to subordinate the interests of the state to his personal sympathies or antipathies."[2]

Realist ideas such as those defended by Bismarck have not always been frowned upon by American leaders; no less a figure than George Washington looked to them for guidance. On April 22, 1792, under political pressure to honor a treaty of alliance with France—then fighting the War of the First Coalition—the president issued a proclamation of neutrality. Against those who protested that morality—faithfulness to treaty obligations and gratitude for aid during the War of Independence—required that the U.S. enter the fray, Alexander Hamilton insisted that the national interest was the final arbiter. According to Hamilton, the rule of morality

> is not precisely the same between nations as between individuals. The duty of making its own welfare the guide of its actions, is much stronger upon the former than upon the latter; in proportion to the greater magnitude and importance of national compared with individual happiness, and to the greater permanency of the effects of national than of individual conduct. Existing millions, and for the most part future generations, are concerned in the present measures of a government; while the consequences of the private actions of an individual ordinarily terminate with himself, or are circumscribed within a narrow compass.[3]

Long before Max Weber made his famous distinction between an ethic of conviction or intention (do what is right!) and an ethic of responsibility, Hamilton pointed to the importance, for a political leader, of considering the likely consequences of his actions.

John Quincy Adams, another astute leader during the Republic's formative years, also belonged to the realist camp— and as a result won Kennan's plaudits. It was Adams who, when secretary of state, let it be known that "America goes not abroad in search of monsters to destroy. She is the well-wisher to the freedom and independence of all. She is the champion and vindicator only of her own. She will recommend the general cause by the countenance of her voice, and the benignant sympathy of her example."[4]

Voices of realism continued to be heard in America after Adams passed from the scene, but as time wore on they were drowned out by those raised on behalf of high-sounding, though abstract, moral principles. When Woodrow Wilson assumed the presidency, he could openly proclaim that politics was nothing but morality and that he intended always to do that which was right. Among those things which were right in his view was that the world be made safe for democracy. As a result, he took the nation into the Great War and set it on a course of intervention that was almost always given moral justification; sometimes that justification was cynical, but not in every case. Wilson's belief, for example, that the Great War pitted good against evil was sincere; it meant that total victory was mandatory—thus prolonging the bloodshed. It was because he had learned nothing from this error that Franklin Roosevelt led the U.S. into another war in which victory became an end in itself and the enemy was forced to surrender unconditionally.

FDR was far from being the only American Wilsonian at the outset of World War II. Virtually all public figures and those for whom they spoke viewed international policy through moral lenses; few remembered the sober counsel offered by Washington, Hamilton, and John Quincy Adams. In part, no doubt, this was due to the messianic strain in American thought, the belief that America had risen above the fallen state of other lands and peoples and thus bore a responsibility to redeem them. It is not surprising, therefore, that a new arrival from the old world had to summon his adopted countrymen back to a prudent realism; his name was Hans Morgenthau.

Morgenthau was born in Coburg, Germany, in 1904; his parents were assimilated Jews. At his father's insistence, he studied law in Frankfurt, Munich, and Berlin. After taking his degree, he served for a time as a legal intern, but the idea of a career in law left him cold. By nature he was attracted to the scholarly life, and when an academic position in German public law opened up in Geneva, he made successful application. He left Germany in 1932, expecting to return when an opportunity presented itself. That he never returned was a result of the fact that, on January 30, 1933, German President Paul von Hindenburg appointed Adolf Hitler chancellor.

For the next few years, Morgenthau and his newly acquired wife moved around Europe. In Geneva he was merely a *Privatdozent* and his income was not enough to satisfy his creditors. In 1935, therefore, he applied for and secured a teaching position in Madrid—little knowing that in a year's time civil war would erupt and, because he was a German citizen, the Republican government would confiscate everything he owned. Until they could decide what to do next, the Morgenthaus sought refuge in Paris, where relatives of Mrs. Morgenthau had opened their home. Nearing desperation, they were finally able—thanks to an affidavit of support from another relative—to obtain immigration visas; they set sail for the United States on July 17, 1937.

Having arrived in New York, Morgenthau began a feverish search for employment; had an instructor at Brooklyn College not fallen ill, he might never have resumed his academic career. The position paid little and when, in 1938, he learned of an opening at the University of Kansas City, he moved to the nation's heartland, where the pay was better but the teaching load was exploitative. As an outspoken critic of the university's president, Morgenthau found himself in bad odor, and at the conclusion of the 1942–43 academic year he received notice that his services would no longer be required. The search for a new position began immediately and ended when the University of Chicago offered him what was initially a temporary position in its political science department. Once on the Windy City's South Side, however, Morgenthau quickly secured a regular appointment.

Free at last from concerns about his professional and financial future, Morgenthau was able to concentrate on what would become his life's work; in a series of influential volumes, he presented a carefully reasoned case for political realism. Happy to have found a new home in America, he declared himself appalled by what he called the country's "intoxication with moral abstractions,"[5] a condition made worse by Woodrow Wilson, for whom considerations of the national interest were immoral. In a section of *In Defense of the National Interest* (1951) titled "The Moral Dignity of the National Interest," Morgenthau attempted to prove the professorial chief executive wrong.

The actual choice, Morgenthau wrote, was "not between moral principles and the national interest . . . but between one set of moral principles divorced from political reality, and another set of moral principles derived from political reality."[6] To be meaningful in an international context, moral principles, he argued, had to move from the abstract to the concrete; what they required could not be decided upon without constant reference to the circumstances on which they were being brought to bear. There being no universally recognized moral code, it was incumbent upon each state to frame its moral judgments with an eye to protecting its—that is its citizens'—vital interests and, indeed, its very existence. Such a view argued for moderation and ruled out moral crusades that, because they allowed for no compromise, found it all but impossible to stop short of the total reduction of an enemy.

Behind what Burke called "the delusive plausibilities of moral politicians,"[7] Morgenthau discerned a streak of utopianism. Such a streak was certainly present in Wilson but so was it also in FDR, who viewed the postwar United Nations as a substitute for balance-of-power politics, a forum in which power struggles would be replaced by cooperation in the creation of a just and peaceful world and thanks to which *national* interest would be superseded once and for all by *global* interest.

Legalism seemed to flow from such utopian notions. Almost invariably, Morgenthau believed, the United States mistook legal agreements and arrangements for realities. Hence the shock that Americans experienced when the Soviet Union violated the Yalta agreement, according to which democratic governments were to be established in Eastern Europe on the basis of free elections. As Morgenthau pointed out, Yalta was doomed from the beginning because the USSR was in military possession of the region. "To invoke against the stark fact of Russian military domination the abstract principle of co-operation and the ideal of universal democracy was as noble in motivation as it was futile as a political act."[8]

Once disillusioned by predictable—that is self-interested—Soviet behavior, Americans began to see themselves engaged in another moral, rather than political, struggle. The Truman Doctrine of 1947 was one of the results. Like Kennan, Morgenthau objected not to the extension of aid to Greece and Turkey but to the doctrine's open-ended character. "Upon what in its immediate import was a limited request for a limited purpose, the Truman Doctrine erected a message of salvation to all the world, unlimited in purpose, unlimited in commitments, and limited in its scope only by the needs of those who would benefit."[9]

Recognizing in Morgenthau a kindred spirit, Kennan invited him to appear before the Policy Planning Staff as a consultant. In the years that followed he continued to benefit from the German-born scholar's wisdom; witness a letter of December 6, 1966, in which he raised a point of disagreement with Morgenthau but quickly added that he "read with great admiration nine-tenths of what appears from your pen."[10] He might have said something similar to Reinhold Niebuhr, the Protestant theologian and social philosopher who had greatly stimulated Morgenthau's thought.

"You are indeed right in surmising that Reinhold Niebuhr's writings have made a profound impression on me," Morgenthau wrote to an interested inquirer on January 11, 1954. "They have confirmed certain conclusions at which I arrived independently and have contributed to deepening and stimulating my thinking."[11] That was also true of Kennan, who devoted one of his Belgrade sermons to Niebuhr. "I thought," he told his flock on that occasion, "I would take these moments this morning to say a few words about the theology and the political philosophy of a man to whose perceptions and thinking I feel myself more indebted than to those of any other person of our time: namely, Reinhold Niebuhr."[12]

Niebuhr's father, Gustav, immigrated to America from Germany in 1881. Soon after his arrival in the new world, he enrolled at Eden Seminary in St. Louis, married, and, in obedience to the Home Mission Board of the Deutsche Evangelische Synode von Nord-Amerika, answered a call to a church in Wright City, Missouri. There, in Middle America, Reinhold and his almost equally well-known brother H. Richard Niebuhr were born. Having decided to follow in his father's footsteps, Reinhold attended Elmhurst College in Illinois before moving on to Eden Seminary; in the summer of 1913, he graduated and was promptly ordained. Seeking a broader education, he then entered Yale's Divinity School, where, in 1914, he earned his degree. The following year Yale University conferred upon him the degree of master of arts.

Upon the completion of his studies at Yale, the German Evangelical Synod assigned Niebuhr to Detroit's Evangelical Church, where he served until 1928. When he began his pastorate, he was already a liberal Protestant for whom social reconstruction was at least as important as personal salvation. Living in the automobile industry's capital, he took up the cause of workers and embraced socialism, an ideology from which he distanced himself only over time. Feeling constrained by his pastoral duties, he accepted an academic appointment at New York's Union Theological Seminary in 1928; there he remained until he retired in 1960.

It is only partly true, as his biographer Richard Wightman Fox maintains, that Niebuhr remained in the camp of liberal Protestantism. He did not believe in individual immortality and had "not the slightest interest in the empty tomb or physical resurrection,"[13] but unlike most liberal Protestants, he could not shake his belief in man's sinful nature. To this belief he gave impressive expression in the Gifford Lectures—"The Nature and Destiny of Man"—that he delivered in Edinburgh in 1939–40.

In the modern liberal Protestant interpretation of Christianity, Niebuhr wrote in the published version of his lectures, "the problem of sin is not understood at all."[14] In his view, liberal Protestants had accommodated themselves too readily to modern culture's optimism concerning human nature. In opposition to that optimism, Niebuhr set Christian realism, a view of man that, while eschewing despair and acknowledging the good of which men were capable, took seriously their capacity for evil. That capacity was a result of original sin, which Niebuhr did not understand as an inheritance from Adam or a factor that relieved men of their responsibility. It was each man's identity with Adam's nature that made sin inevitable—yet not necessary.

Niebuhr conceded that there was a paradox at the heart of the doctrine of original sin, but he gave to it as clear an explanation as it is probably possible to give when he wrote the following: "The essence of man is his freedom. Sin is committed in that freedom. Sin can therefore not be attributed to a defect in his essence. It can only be understood as a self-contradiction, made possible by the fact of his freedom but not following necessarily from it."[15]

However difficult for reason the doctrine of original sin might be, the record of human history witnessed to its essential validity, a view shared by all political realists, whatever their religious beliefs. Without doubt, it was Niebuhr's chastened view of human nature that allied him with the realists. It certainly made an impression upon Kennan. No wonder, then, that he read Niebuhr's *Irony of American History* (1952) with the greatest interest.

Kennan responded favorably to Niebuhr's observations, in that important work, that "even the best human actions involve some guilt" and that Americans deceived themselves by believing that they could act as tutors of mankind "in its pilgrimage to perfection."[16] Unable or unwilling to confront the ironies of their own history—virtues that too easily became vices, strengths that became weaknesses, wisdom that became folly—they refused to recognize the limits proper to finite beings. "The ironic elements in American history can be overcome," Niebuhr concluded, "only if American idealism comes to terms with the limits of all human striving, the fragmentariness of all human wisdom, the precariousness of all historic configurations of power, and the mixture of good and evil in all human virtue."[17]

Kennan could not have agreed more, and he was pleased to note that Niebuhr praised his *American Diplomacy, 1900–1950*

(1951) for its incisive criticism of the nation's foreign policy. Nor did he seem to be disturbed by Niebuhr's mistaken idea that his defense of the national interest was a form of national egotism. Unlike Kennan and Morgenthau, in fact, Niebuhr never accepted the pursuit of the national interest as the proper goal of diplomacy; for him it was merely a description of how states do in fact conduct themselves. Still, there was more than enough wisdom to be found in *The Irony of American History* to commend the book and its author to both realists. Kennan was delighted when Oppenheimer invited Niebuhr to spend 1958 as a visiting member of the Institute for Advanced Study, and he helped the aging theologian with the writing of *The Structure of Nations and Empires* (1959), a work, however, that showed signs of diminishing powers.

In the first volume of his memoirs, Kennan wrote that "intellectually and aesthetically, Germany had made a deep impression on me."[18] He could not, therefore, have been surprised to find that almost all of his fellow realists were German or of German descent. Along with Morgenthau and Niebuhr, one might mention in this regard Walter Lippmann and Henry Kissinger, for both of whom Kennan had the utmost respect. Of the policy of détente pursued by Kissinger and President Nixon, for example, Kennan wrote approvingly that the former Harvard professor "brought to the operation a measure of imagination, boldness of approach, and sophistication of understanding without which it would have been difficult to achieve."[19] And there was, of course, Bismarck, for whom Kennan's admiration was unbounded.

Although he drew intellectual sustenance from these realists, Kennan arrived at his views independently, as a result of his diplomatic experience and historical study. Lacking any taste for abstract discussions or treatises, he usually set forth his view of realism within the context of concrete examinations of concrete problems. Nevertheless, certain of his convictions and principles stand out in bold relief.

Of human limitation he seems always to have been almost painfully aware. As he saw it, man's animal nature set limits to his efforts to lend his existence a greater dignity, order, and elevation than could be found in the lower species. Man, in short, was not perfectible. That fact ruled out all utopian projects, all hope for a world of permanent peace and harmony, and all efforts to remove considerations of power from the diplomatic equation. A prudent foreign policy was one that accepted the realities of power and interest and strove to keep the inevitable conflicts between nations within tolerable limits.

Such a policy could be successful only if it took as its guiding principle the national interest. With respect to the purposes of states—as distinct from the methods, which should always be moral—moral principles could not, according to Kennan, serve as useful (that is, practical) guides, not only because no nation could assume the universal validity or acceptance of its own principles, but also because governments were agents responsible before all else for protecting the interests—the security and well-being—of those whom they represented. It was precisely "man's irrational nature, his selfishness, his obstinacy, his tendency to violence" that rendered government an institution unsuited to give pure expression to morality.[20]

That did not mean, Kennan insisted, that a policy based upon the national interest was immoral. If "we will have the modesty to admit that our own national interest is all that we are really capable of knowing and understanding—and the courage to recognize that if our purposes and undertakings here at home are decent ones, unsullied by arrogance or hostility toward other people or delusions of superiority, then the pursuit of our national interest can never fail to be conducive to a better world."[21]

It has generally been held by realists that the pursuit of the national interest entails a moral double standard; the duties possessed by a private individual cannot simply be carried with him when he assumes responsibility as a leader of government. That does not mean that he can act according to personal caprice or that he is at liberty to pursue his own selfish ends, but it does mean that he cannot be held to strict moral account when to do so would imperil or work to the disadvantage of an entire people. Kennan would certainly have agreed that he could not indulge his own moral enthusiasms, but whether or not he would have approved of morally problematic actions is difficult to say; such approval does seem inescapable if one believes, as he surely did, that public servants are agents rather than principals. There is no doubt, however, that he believed that the pursuit of the national interest had always to be peaceful and constructive.

For Kennan, realism mandated moderation, a sense of proportion, and a recognition of limits. He evinced no sympathy for moral crusades, imperial adventures, or interventions in foreign lands. It was not, in his view, the business of the United States to attempt to determine political developments in other countries; it was certainly not its business to work for the overthrow of a foreign regime. There was, to begin with, the problem of finding a viable alternative. Then too, it was easier to intervene than to find a way out. Only when U.S. interests were seriously and directly imperiled should intervention be contemplated.

But realism meant something else as well: a rejection of any idea of American "exceptionalism" or messianism, any claim that superior virtue placed upon Americans a redemptive burden on a global scale. "Let us not," he wrote in a 1952 letter to the *New York Times,* "attempt to constitute ourselves the guardians of everyone else's virtue; we have enough trouble to guard our own."[22] In *Around the Cragged Hill,* he put it more strongly. "We are, for the love of God, only human beings, the descendants of human beings, the bearers, like our ancestors, of all the usual human frailties."[23] To the best of its ability, then, a chastened America would be well advised to tend its own garden and to seek those accommodations with other countries which helped to maintain a stable, if potentially dangerous and always imperfect, world. This was not isolationism (it was too late for that), but a recognition of limits and a policy of restraint—all the more necessary in the nuclear age.

◆◆◆

One does not have to read much of Kennan's work to recognize that he believed democracy to be inimical to a mature and responsible foreign policy. In the published version of his Oxford lectures of 1957–58, he cited Tocqueville to the effect that "a democracy can only with great difficulty regulate the details of an important undertaking, persevere in a fixed design, and work out its execution in spite of serious obstacles."[24] One reason for that unsteadiness of purpose was that those charged with responsibility for the conduct of foreign policy had to contend with public opinion, which was woefully uninformed and notoriously erratic. Once aroused by war, democratic peoples were subject to seizures of political emotionalism; nothing short of total victory would satisfy them.

Moreover, because democratic governments were persuaded of their own moral superiority, they came to believe that they were duty bound to promote democracy around the world. That sense of responsibility created in their leaders an interventionist mentality that often distorted their judgment. It was by no means clear, Kennan believed, that democracy possessed universal validity, that it was the form of government best suited to all peoples at all times. In fact, world history knew of relatively few democracies in the modern sense of the word; they were limited in both time and space. The claim advanced by many Americans that all peoples would prosper under democratic rule had to be viewed with suspicion.

And so should all talk of "human rights," said to be discoverable by reason and universally binding. The notion of rights "remote from human authorship," Kennan did not hesitate to say, "leads me into philosophical thickets where I cannot follow."[25] While he could understand human rights as ideal projections of Western liberal principles, he could not conceive of them as already existing in the absence of a granting authority, an enforcing agency, and a set of corresponding duties. Moreover, as a Christian, he could not see how, before his Creator, he could assert a "right" to anything. He would instead hope for God's mercy.

But even if global democracy were a worthy policy goal, Kennan felt little confidence in the ability of U.S. leaders to achieve it. For one thing, all those clamoring for democracy seemed to be highly selective in the countries they identified as being in need of America's ministrations. It always seemed to be right-wing authoritarianism that sparked their moral outrage; left-wing tyrannies failed to inspire the same crusading zeal. As he put it to George Urban, the splendid Hungarian-born interviewer: "Any régime that chooses to call itself Marxist can be sure that its brutalities and oppression will be forgiven, whereas any régime that does not is stamped as being of the Right, in which case the slightest invasion of the rights or liberties of the individual on *its* territory at once becomes the object of intense indignation."[26]

Then there was the naïve American belief according to which all who claim to be fighting for democracy and freedom would, once in power, institutionalize democracy and freedom. More likely, Kennan believed, "freedom fighters" were looking forward to the day when they could torment those who had tormented them. In a society that had been subjected to tyrannical rule, it was always difficult for anyone, whatever his intentions, to govern by methods strikingly different from those to which people had become accustomed. Kennan recalled the efforts of his namesake, the author of *Siberia and the Exile System,* to rally support for Russia's revolutionaries—his assumption being that, in power, their rule would prove to be morally and politically superior to that of the tsar. "Have we learned anything from this lesson?" Kennan asked rhetorically.[27]

But Kennan's criticism of democracy was not limited to its adverse effect upon foreign policy. Although he occasionally expressed a resigned allegiance to political democracy, he clearly sympathized with the tradition of antidemocratic thought that reaches back to Plato. In the *Republic,* the great philosopher was willing to concede that tyranny was worse than democracy, though not much worse. Burke allowed that "there may be situations in which the purely democratic form will become necessary. There may be some (very few, and very particularly circumstanced) where it would be clearly desireable."[28] Very particularly circumstanced indeed. Like most thinkers of Kennan's admired eighteenth century—including *philosophes* such as Voltaire and Diderot—he was hostile to democracy. So, for that matter, were America's founding fathers.

Tocqueville, for whom Kennan felt a particular affinity, gave democracy credit where he thought it due—for its introduction into the family of greater affection, for instance—but his overall assessment was decidedly negative. In the French aristocrat's view, democracy equaled equality, social as well as political. And equality meant the centralization of power, because only national government could impose uniform conditions upon an entire people; those lobbying for egalitarian measures would therefore demand the introduction of new national laws and a corresponding increase in national authority.

Such demands would increase the threat of tyranny. Not only would power rest in fewer hands, but each new step in the direction of equality would lead to greater restrictions upon liberty. That was so because equality had to be coerced; those above the line would not willingly lower themselves to it. Nor was that all. Tocqueville also argued that democracies would elevate to power men of inferior rank, and that education, in its striving to be universal, would inevitably tend toward mediocrity.

If anything, Kennan's view of egalitarianism was even more jaundiced than Tocqueville's. In part that was a result of having observed life in the Soviet Union. While most Soviet citizens lived in economic misery, they consoled themselves with the thought that their plight was shared by the majority of those around them. The main thing for them and for the more radical champions of the redistributive state

> was that no one should live better than anyone else. Uniformity was an end in itself. If your style of living deviated from it downwards . . . this was nothing discreditable; it was merely a sign that you were unjustly deprived, and deserved greater benefits from the state. To deviate from it upwards, however, or at least to show signs of doing so, was reprehensible. It was a sign that you were depriving someone else of something, and ought not to be tolerated.[29]

Like other critics of democracy, then, Kennan viewed the passion for equality as the product of envy and resentment. These base discontents were aroused particularly by the privilege of birth, making it impossible for those who experienced them to appreciate the wisdom of Gibbon, whom Kennan often cited to the effect that "the superior prerogative of birth, when it is sanctioned by time and experience, is the plainest and least invidious of the distinctions between mankind."[30] But Kennan

143

went well beyond that obvious truth to make the case for privilege even when those advantaged were not particularly worthy. His argument, which he knew would outrage modern sensibilities, was as thoughtful as it was convincing.

During a visit to Leningrad in the early 1970s, he stood in front of what, during tsarist times, had been the Imperial Yacht Club. His thoughts turned to the meals that had once been eaten there, the wines drunk, and he wondered

> whether it did not actually add something of color and variety to the city for the people of that day to know that here, in these premises, there was being prepared, even if they didn't eat it, some of the finest food eaten anywhere in northern Europe, that here things were being done elegantly, impressively, to the connoisseur's taste. Is there, in other words, not a certain reassurance, a certain twinge of hope, to be derived from the reflection that someone, at least, in the place you inhabit, even if it is not you, lives well, from the knowledge that to live well is at least theoretically a possibility?[31]

What mattered to Kennan was not whether or not the privileged were deserving, though of course it would be nice if they were. What mattered was the existence of civilized ways of life that set a tone, an aspiration for society. As he once told members of the Congress for Cultural Freedom, "I simply shudder to think of a world in which life is *nowhere* led with grace and distinction, where *no one* has the privilege of privacy and quietude, in which *nowhere* is true excellence cultivated for its own sake."[32] Clearly he assumed that there *were* better and worse ways of living, that the notion that nothing was better or worse "but only different" was false and pernicious, and that the principle of hierarchy was indispensable to the maintenance of civilization.

Opposition to hierarchy was, in Kennan's view, opposition to civilized life. "I am anything but an egalitarian," he told Eric Sevareid in 1975. "I am very much opposed to egalitarian tendencies of all sorts in governmental life and in other walks of life. Sometimes I've been charged with being an elitist. Well, of course, I am. What do people expect? God forbid that we should be without an elite. Is everything to be done by gray mediocrity?"[33] Men were equal in dignity, but in nothing else; to pretend otherwise was to insult intelligence.

The closer one looks at Kennan's view of governments, democratic and nondemocratic, the clearer it becomes that had there been a choice, he would have opted for a government of a conservative authoritarian type—"the norm," he pointed out, "of Western society in the Christian era." There was a good reason for that: "The authoritarian regime, despite its origins and its sanctions, often rests on a wide area of popular acceptance and reflects popular aspirations in important degree."[34] Recall that he once composed a paper titled "The Prerequisites: Notes on Problems of the United States in 1938," in which he argued for changes leading to an "authoritarian state," much like that presided over by Austria's Kurt von Schuschnigg.

He was later to describe that government as "conservative, semifascist, but still moderate" and to complain that those in the West who criticized it "found it hard to distinguish between traditional conservatives and Nazis."[35] He was not himself wholly uncritical of the Schuschnigg government; in a personal letter (to whom he did not say) that he wrote from Prague on December 8, 1938, he called unfavorable attention to its disapproval of democracy, though it is unlikely that he was being perfectly honest. In any event, he concluded with a favorable estimate: "[T]he Schuschnigg regime was not a bad thing for Austria."[36]

For one thing, as we have seen, he admired the way in which the regime relied upon a committee of experts to reform Austria's social-insurance system.

There seemed to be little doubt [he later observed] that if malicious despotism had greater possibilities for evil than democracy, benevolent despotism likewise had greater possibilities for good. An intelligent, determined ruling minority, responsible in a general sense to the people at large rather than in a direct sense to groups of politicians and lobbyists or to the voters of individual districts, could function not only more efficiently but also, when it wished to, more beneficially than could the average "democratic" regime.[37]

During the war, he negotiated with António de Oliveira Salazar and came away with a favorable impression. Unlike many of his countrymen, he recognized that Salazar was a traditional authoritarian, not a fascist revolutionary. A fascist dictatorship, the Portuguese leader once said, leaned "towards a pagan Caesarism, towards a new state which recognizes no limitations of legal or moral order."[38] Salazar never adopted the trappings of fascism—chanting crowds, mass meetings, the cult of personality; he was, in fact, a recluse. Nor did he amass personal wealth while exercising power.

Salazar did take advantage of his country's wolfram (tungsten) resource by selling it to both Allies and Germans during the war, but he was trying to maintain Portuguese neutrality, and he sympathized with the war against the Soviet Union because he regarded communism as the greatest threat to Europe. Nevertheless, he recognized the similarities between international and national socialism: "Although Fascism and National Socialism differ from Communism in economic outlook and ideas, they are alike in their conception of the totalitarian state."[39] And he did, after all, lease bases in the Azores to the Allies.

Like those authoritarian leaders whom he respected, Kennan looked with distaste upon mass politics. "For years," he wrote in the late 1960s, "Gibbon's dictum 'Under a democratical government the citizens exercise the powers of sovereignty; and those powers will be first abused [sic; "abased" was Gibbon's word], and afterwards lost, if they are committed to an unwieldy multitude' has lain at the heart of my political philosophy."[40] Whether or not he ever read *The Revolt of the Masses* (1930), he shared the views of José Ortega y Gasset, the right-wing liberal who made an important distinction between mass men and select individuals, between those who demand much of themselves and those who demand little or nothing. It was men of the latter sort, according to Ortega, who in the twentieth century were asserting their right to mediocrity and who attempted to crush everything outstanding, excellent, and noble.

Kennan was too much the realist to think that America might begin to question democratic ideology; like Tocqueville, he hoped only to hold its most damaging aspects in check. Whenever he could, he made the case for professionalism in politics, for a special advisory role for men and women of proven ability and maturity of judgment, members of an elite who demanded much of themselves. Such people, he argued, should be shielded from the whims and pressures of public opinion and from the vulgar requirements of seeking elected office. In other words, they should not be held hostage to public-opinion polls. In that way, he hoped, the weaknesses of democracy might be mitigated.

In 1978, the Ethics and Public Policy Center in Washington published a collection of papers titled *Decline of the West? George Kennan and His Critics.* The title was well chosen, because as the years passed Kennan did adopt an ever more pessimistic attitude with respect to the West's future. Often, he must have thought back to the summer before he reported for duty with the foreign service—the year was 1926—when he read Spengler's *Untergang des Abendlandes,* a book that left a permanent mark upon him, as it did upon so many other thoughtful people. Thomas Mann thought it the most important book of the era, and Ludwig Wittgenstein recognized that its cultural pessimism held important implications for his own thinking.

Spengler distinguished between a *Kultur* (a civilization in its fullness) and a *Zivilization* (its dying or decadent stage). Each *Kultur*—Spengler identified eight in world history—had a life span of about one thousand years. Western *Kultur,* the beginning of which Spengler placed at around 1000 A.D., would therefore be dead *inwardly* by around 2000. The signs of decline were already there to see in the nineteenth century, a century that Kennan viewed as inferior to that which preceded it. *Kultur und Zivilization,* Spengler wrote, are "the living body of a soul and the mummy of it. For Western existence the distinction lies at about the year 1800—on the one side of that frontier life in fullness and sureness of itself, formed by growth from within, in one great uninterrupted evolution from Gothic childhood to Goethe and Napoleon, and on the other the autumnal, artificial, rootless life of our great cities, under forms fashioned by the intellect."[41]

Spengler's view that the eighteenth century represented the high point of Western *Kultur* could not but appeal to Kennan. So did the German's identification of world cities—metropolises—with decadent *Zivilization.* They produced "a new sort of nomad, cohering unstably in fluid masses, the parasitical city dweller, traditionless, utterly matter-of-fact, religionless, clever, unfruitful, deeply contemptuous of the countryman and especially that highest form of countryman, the country gentleman."[42] The city dweller was contemptuous of someone, that is, like Kennan.

Although Spengler did not cite Gibbon, he did say that the decline of the West was "analogous" to the decline of Rome; the ancient city provided the key to understanding the future. How-

ever much the surface details of the empire's decline might differ from those of the West, the two developments were "entirely
similar as regards the inward power driving the great organism
towards its end."[43]

One of the signs that Western man sensed what fate awaited
his *Kultur* was his "wistful regard" for ruins. "We . . . are moved
by a secret piety to preserve the aqueducts of the Campagna,
the Etruscan tombs, the ruins of Luxor and Karnak, the crum-
bling castles of the Rhine, the Roman Limes, Hersfeld and
Paulinzella from becoming mere rubbish—but we keep them
*as ruins,* feeling in some subtle way that reconstruction would
deprive them of something, indefinable in terms, that can never
be reproduced."[44] Such ruins serve as reminders of the inevitable decay of the works of human hands.

"It was," Gibbon wrote in his *Autobiography* (1796), "at Rome,
on the fifteenth of October, 1764, as I sat musing amidst the
ruins of the Capitol, while the barefooted fryars were singing
vespers in the temple of Jupiter, that the idea of writing the decline and fall of the City first started to my mind."[45] He began
his magisterial *History of the Decline and Fall of the Roman Empire*
with this famous sentence: "In the second century of the Christian Æra, the empire of Rome comprehended the fairest part
of the earth, and the most civilized portion of mankind."[46] The
empire was then at its peak, thanks to the spirit of *moderation*
with which Augustus had imbued it.

For Gibbon, the enlightened historian, excess or immoderation of any kind was anathema. That is why he praised Augustus
for resting content with the republic's conquests, for forswearing
any idea of subduing the entire world. "Inclined to peace by
his temper and situation, it was easy for him to discover, that
Rome, in her present exalted situation, had much less to hope
than to fear from the chance of arms."[47]

Not all of Augustus's successors followed his example, but
some, like Hadrian and the two Antonines—Antoninus Pius

and Marcus Aurelius Antoninus—did. Gibbon expressed his admiration for the prudence and moderation of Hadrian (ruled A.D. 117–38), in whom there was no trace of the martial and ambitious spirit that animated his predecessor, Trajan; during his reign, Rome enjoyed peace and prosperity. He and the Antonines (ruled A.D. 138–80) maintained the dignity and integrity of the empire without attempting to expand its frontiers. Moreover, each of them tolerated religions of virtually every kind. According to Gibbon, it was their moderate and tolerant approach to governing that raised the empire to the heights.

What, then, caused the empire to fall from those heights? The barbarian invasions? They simply delivered the coup de grâce. The rise of Christianity to the status of state religion? Yes, although that was only the most important aspect of a more encompassing cause. Gibbon put his view most succinctly in the famous section titled "General Observations on the Fall of the Roman Empire in the West": "The decline of Rome was the natural and inevitable effect of immoderate greatness."[48] Too much ambition; too much prosperity; too much power in the hands of the Prætorian guards; too many provincials bearing the name "Roman" who knew nothing of the Roman spirit— these were the causes of destruction.

Above all, in Gibbon's view, the decline and fall resulted from Christian immoderation. In the famous—or infamous— chapters 15 and 16 (and elsewhere), the great historian made no attempt to express himself in moderate terms. The early Christians, he conceded, were simple and mild folk, but from the first they preached and practiced an intolerant exclusivity. Whereas the pagans stood ready to add another god to the pantheon, the followers of Christ insisted that theirs was the only God. Gibbon was a nonbeliever, and in his view religion of any kind was for the ignorant and superstitious masses. Those of a sophisticated and philosophic cast of mind—those like Gibbon himself—recognized the social usefulness of religion, but only when it was polytheistic, tolerant, moderate in its enthusiasm, and modest in its claims.

Christianity was none of those things. Christians were immoderately passive; they discouraged the active virtues and buried the last remains of military spirit in the cloister. For monks, indeed, Gibbon reserved a particular animosity: "The sacred indolence of the monks was devoutly embraced by a servile and effeminate age."[49] At the same time, however, Gibbon viewed Christians as immoderately pugnacious; even within their own camp, zealotry could not be held in check. Between the bishops of Rome and those of the provinces, for example, there was cold war. If that war was carried on "without any effusion of blood," Gibbon observed, "it was owing much less to the moderation than to the weakness of the contending prelates."[50] Like almost all Christians, the bishops were fanatics who for a variety of reasons—zeal, the promise of another world, miraculous claims, rigid virtue, church organization—were able to transform themselves from a persecuted minority into an intolerant majority.

Christians had been persecuted, yes, but Gibbon insisted that pagan treatment of them was less intolerable than many believed. He conceded that Nero may have carried things too far, but Christians were always so obstinate, so unanimous in their refusal to hold any communion with the pagan gods. What is more, once *they* came to power they were "no less diligently employed in displaying the cruelty, than in imitating the conduct, of their Pagan adversaries."[51]

Of Constantine, the emperor who made Christianity the religion of the empire, Gibbon had little good to report. He was, the historian maintained, a cruel and dissolute ruler who hastened the fall of the empire, not least by promulgating a law "by which the exercise of the pagan worship was absolutely suppressed, and a considerable part of his subjects was left destitute of priests, of temples, and of any public religion."[52] He was, as this and other of his actions attested, an immoderate man.

Not so Julian, called the Apostate, the emperor who attempted in vain to restore paganism. Unlike Constantine, Julian was
moderate and tolerant; "the only hardship which he inflicted on
the Christians, was to deprive them of the power of tormenting
their fellow-subjects, whom they stigmatized with the odious
titles of idolaters and heretics."[53] If any blame attached to him
it was due to the fact that he was a true believer in the pagan
gods and not a philosophic skeptic concerning all religion. In
Gibbon's view, he should have emulated those who had allowed
philosophy to purify "their minds from the prejudices of the
popular superstition" and who therefore rejected Christianity:
Seneca, the elder and younger Pliny, Tacitus, Plutarch, Galen,
Epictetus, Marcus Aurelius.

Having recounted his melancholy tale of Rome's decline
and fall, Gibbon asked if it contained a warning to the present.
Might Europe one day suffer a similar fate? He thought not. In
one of Kennan's favorite passages, he wrote that

> the abuses of tyranny are restrained by the mutual influ-
> ence of fear and shame; republics have acquired order and
> stability; monarchies have imbibed the principles of free-
> dom, or, at least, of moderation; and some sense of hon-
> our and justice is introduced into the most defective con-
> stitutions by the general manner of the times. In peace,
> the progress of knowledge and industry is accelerated by
> the emulation of so many active rivals: in war, the Eu-
> ropean forces are exercised by temperate and indecisive
> contests.[54]

All in all, the human species was marching toward perfection.

It did not seem so to Kennan. On a ship leaving Southhamp-
ton in 1959, he looked out at the shoreline and saw remainders
"of a civilization that not long ago (within the memory of living
man) seemed, and believed itself to be, of a solidity unequaled

since the days of the Roman Empire, and is yet today so wholly undermined that almost nothing remains of it except in the universities, in the pretenses or habits of a few older people, and in [some] physical Victorian relics."[55]

Unlike Gibbon, of course, Kennan had lived through the Great War, the event that he believed lay at the heart of the decline of Western civilization. For him as for so many other members of his generation, the war changed everything. The title of Robert Graves's famous autobiography, *Good-bye to All That* (1929), could have been chosen by anyone who had known life before and after the catastrophe (though Graves's title referred to his decision, after a failed marriage, to leave England for Majorca). "Things fall apart," W. B. Yeats wrote in "The Second Coming" (written in January 1919), "the centre cannot hold."

"There died a myriad," Ezra Pound lamented in 1920, "And of the best, among them / For an old bitch gone in the teeth / For a botched civilization." Pound then edited the poem by T. S. Eliot that came to stand as the great metaphor for postwar Western civilization: *The Waste Land* (1922). No doubt Kennan had that metaphor in mind as he visited the ruins of an Estonian cathedral in 1929, roamed through Libau's ruined factory district in 1932, and stood amid East Berlin's ruins in 1960.

Later in the decade, we know, Kennan confronted the threat posed by student radicals to what remained of Western civilization. He answered them and their supporters in great detail and, in the summer of 1968, delivered a sober address in colonial Williamsburg on "America After Vietnam." He spoke of violent protests, of "the spectacle of angry and disorderly people: milling about, chanting, screaming, shouting other people down, brawling with the police or with equally violent opponents, obstructing other people in their normal pursuits." Taking his cue from Tocqueville, he reminded his audience that in order to remain loyal to the principles upon which it was founded,

America required a broad community of political and cultural understanding. He warned against throwing the country open to "the immigration of great masses of people reared in quite different climates of political and ethical principle."[56]

Kennan emphasized that he was not talking about ethnic or racial differences, but about differences in culture. He was thus among the first to sound an alarm concerning immigration policies that had the effect of undermining the cultural tradition upon which the nation's identity, in fact its very existence, depended. As he spoke, he may have had in mind what Gibbon had written about provincials who received the name "Roman" without understanding or adopting the Roman spirit.

Kennan lived long enough to witness the invasion—there is no other word for it—of the Southwest and the refusal of the national government to enforce immigration laws. In 2000, he said to a *New Yorker* interviewer, "I think the country is coming apart, partly because of its susceptibility to immigration";[57] and he devoted a section of *Around the Cragged Hill* to that critical issue. Because, he wrote, America was a nation of immigrants, many Americans had come to assume that there was no limit either to the number of immigrants or to the diversity of ethnic characteristics the country could accept. But while America might be a large country, it could not open its borders to all those, many of whom came from a background of poverty, who wished to enter.

To do so would be to risk replicating in the United States those conditions which obtained in the lands from which the immigrants had taken flight. Cheap labor might seem attractive to businesses, but a dependence on it could prove fatal to American civilization. Kennan warned that such dependence, "like the weakness of the Romans in allowing themselves to become dependent on the barbarians to fill the ranks of their own armies, can become, if not checked betimes, the beginning of the end." He thought it inexplicable that the U.S. government could put hundreds of thousands of troops in the Near East to expel Saddam Hussein from Kuwait, while confessing "itself unable to defend its own southwestern border from illegal immigration by large numbers of people armed with nothing more formidable than a strong desire to get across it."[58]

Kennan knew that, like many Muslims in Europe, most of the invaders of the United States arrived without any intention of assimilating; quite the contrary, they expected Americans to accommodate their language and culture. Other critics have begun to echo Kennan's warning. "We are witnessing," Patrick Buchanan has written, "how nations perish. We are entered upon the final act of our civilization. The last scene is the deconstruction of the nations. The penultimate scene, now well underway, is the invasion unresisted."[59]

The invasion of millions of unassimilated and unassimilable human beings was not the only sign of decline that Kennan perceived. He spoke with unconcealed disgust of pandemic crime, the widespread use of narcotics, the deterioration of educational standards, the decay of cities, the ubiquity of pornography, and the thoughtless exploitation of nature. He was not joking when, in 1976, he told George Urban about a recent summer cruise in the Baltic: "I put in at a small Danish port which was having a youth festival. The place was swarming with hippies—motorbikes, girl-friends, drugs, pornography, drunkenness, noise—it was all there. I looked at this mob and thought how one company of robust Russian infantry would drive it out of town."[60]

The following year, on a ferry headed for Denmark, Kennan could not help but think, as he looked at the young Europeans aboard, of the intellectual and spiritual vacuum that the European welfare state had produced. Things were no better in the United States. In Florida in 1984, he gazed at the small homes that lined an artificially created canal. They were modern and tidy, but he could not believe in their permanence. In his mind's eye, he saw them in ruins, victims of hurricanes, insects, "and the ultimate collapse of civilization as we know it."[61]

Not only civilization but life itself, Kennan argued, was endangered by environmental deterioration—only nuclear weapons posed a greater threat to the future of mankind. Rarely did he miss an opportunity to issue apocalyptic warnings or to lobby for draconian measures to protect the natural world. His devotion to this cause was religious in character. "For young people, the world over," he wrote in 1970, "some new opening of hope and creativity is becoming an urgent spiritual necessity."[62] Twenty-five years later he asked whether there was not, "whatever the nature of one's particular God, an element of sacrilege involved in the placing of all this [that is, the earth and its beauty] at stake just for the sake of the comforts, the fears, and the national rivalries of a single generation?"[63]

Kennan had always loved nature and deplored its heedless and unnecessary exploitation, but during the 1950s his alarm at the harm men were doing began to grow. We know that he read and admired *The Sea Around Us* (1951), Rachel Carson's scientific and yet beautifully poetic guide to what was known and what remained mysterious about the majestic oceans that surround and make life possible for man. He must have been moved by Carson's loving portrait of the seas, for which he felt an almost mystical bond. Whenever possible, he chose the ocean liner over the airplane—at sea he could be reminded of what civilized travel had once been. And there was something more. He could have written what Carson did write:

> In the artificial world of his cities and towns, [man] often forgets the true nature of his planet and the long vistas of its history, in which the existence of the race of men has occupied a mere moment of time. The sense of all these things comes to him most clearly in the course of a long ocean voyage, when he watches day after day the receding

rim of the horizon, ridged and furrowed by waves; when at night he becomes aware of the earth's rotation as the stars pass overhead; or when, alone in this world of water and sky, he feels the loneliness of his earth in space.[64]

At the helm of the *Nagawicka,* he sailed the Scandinavian waters and derived pleasure from the peace found far from the madding crowd. He was an old-fashioned man and at heart an old-fashioned conservationist, not an ideological environmentalist. In this way, he had much in common with Wendell Berry, the Kentucky farmer/agrarian and writer who left New York University to return to his rural roots. Berry believes that there are two ways of approaching nature—as exploiter or as "nurturer." The former is a specialist; the latter is not. The standard of the exploiter is efficiency; the standard of the nurturer is care. The goal of the exploiter is money; the goal of the nurturer is health—that of the land, family, community, country, and self.[65] Whether or not he was familiar with Berry's work, Kennan would certainly have agreed.

As he was aware of the importance of solar activity and remembered what Carson wrote about "the ocean [as] the great regulator, the great stabilizer of temperatures,"[66] it is not likely that Kennan would have credited apocalyptic claims concerning "global warming" and man's responsibility for it. Still, he did sometimes give in to visions of doom and advocate extreme means of control. In order "to prevent a world wasteland," the title of a 1970 piece for *Foreign Affairs,* he proposed the creation of an "International Environmental Agency" composed of scientists and experts who would set aside the interests of their own countries and act only in the interest of mankind. "It is," he assured readers, "not a question here of giving orders, exerting authority or telling governments what to do."[67]

But of course that is exactly what the agency would be charged with doing. Kennan's growing, and perfectly legitimate, concern over the thoughtless and irresponsible exploitation of nature threw him into the arms of those for whom environmentalism aimed less at conservation than at reconstructing the social order along socialist lines. He certainly knew that it is one thing to exercise authority within national frontiers and quite another to do so internationally.

International cooperation that is not voluntary must run an enormous risk of tyranny, for in the political atmosphere of the contemporary world it is unlikely that "environmental statesmen and diplomats [and] true international servants" without a political agenda could be found. Moreover, experience has shown that an international and bureaucratic tyranny would take aim primarily at the Western nations. Non-Western nations would receive passes, even when they were clearly guilty of polluting and other sins against the natural world. In retrospect, Kennan was also excessively optimistic about the role that communist nations could be expected to play.

Kennan's indictment of the exploitation of nature was only the most obvious sign of his deepening pessimism concerning the West's future. Not surprisingly, he preferred to look back upon earlier times. In a series of lectures that he delivered at Princeton University in the early 1950s, he recalled with affection the America he knew as a boy. "Our national myth relates," he told his audience, "to an America which has long since ceased to be the real and dominant one. It relates to a rural America, an unmechanical America, an America without motor cars and television sets, an America of the barefoot boy and the whitewashed board fence, the America of the Webster cartoon. It was a wonderful old America. I sometimes wonder whether those of us who knew it will ever really adjust to any other."[68]

Kennan felt much the same way about the old Europe. In a diary entry that he made in Hamburg in December 1927, he expressed regret that he had not lived fifty or a hundred years earlier. "We know too many cities to be able to grow into any of them. . . . We have too many friends to have any friendships, too many books to know any of them well. . . . I should like to have lived in the days when a visit was a matter of months . . . when foreign countries were still foreign, when a vast part of the world always bore the glamour of the great unknown."[69]

In the summer of 1956, on a train from Chicago to St. Louis, Kennan thought he saw the present age as his father might view it from the grave: "blind, willful, doomed, and not very interesting. I am living in the world my father despaired of, and rightly so." It was the past that he loved, but to try to explain why to contemporaries would be futile. "We of the past," he wrote, "have a secret; and we need never worry about its being betrayed—for no one now is curious about it. No one would understand it even if he tried."[70]

That Kennan was a cultural pessimist there is no doubt, but he stopped short of counseling despair; he would never have expressed Spengler's hope "that men of the new generation may be moved by this book to devote themselves to technics instead of lyrics, the sea instead of the paint-brush, and politics instead of epistemology."[71] As the motto for the epilogue to *Around the Cragged Hill,* he chose the words of the wizard Gandalf in J. R. R. Tolkien's *Fellowship of the Ring*: "Despair is only for those who see the end beyond all doubt."[72]

However pessimistic Kennan was concerning the future of Western civilization, his Christian faith made him tremble at the thought of destroying all hope among his readers. That would be, he wrote, "the unpardonable sin. The hour may be late, but there is nothing that says that it is too late."[73] We know that he meant what he said because he gave so much of himself in an effort to steer the United States and the entire West in new—or rather old—and more promising directions. In a sermon titled "Why Do I Hope," delivered at Princeton University's beautiful chapel, he declared life to be good, especially when lived in harmony with nature.

Kennan may not have been aware of the fact that Tolkien had fought at the Somme, one of the Great War's most horrific battles, and that by 1918 had lost all but one of his close friends; Tolkien knew suffering and loss. And yet, unlike so many of those who fought and survived, or who simply experienced the war from afar, he never surrendered to disenchantment and despair. His friend of later years, C. S. Lewis, called *The Lord of the Rings* (1954–55) "a recall from facile optimism and wailing pessimism alike" that presides at "the cool middle point between illusion and disillusionment."[74] That is undoubtedly why Kennan felt so drawn to Tolkien's epic work of the imagination.

Kennan always described himself as a conservative, even a "profound" conservative. It began with dress. On the dust jacket of *Around the Cragged Hill,* there is a photograph of him in a pinstriped suit and vest, polka-dot tie, and pocketsquare—the very picture of formality. The casual dress favored by most Americans was not for him; nor could he approve of social informality. Such things were very much out of place in the diplomatic world, and in Kennan's view rightly so. Manners betokened breeding and bestowed dignity. Good form was not something snobbish and unnecessary; it elevated men above animal existence and relieved them of the burden of having to create their own social universe. And that is not all.

> Some of us are inclined to feel [Kennan told a University of Virginia audience in 1947] that even in international affairs the observance of good form and good manners has probably done more in the end for civilized and peaceful living than all the moralizing about the content of human behavior. What is important, in other words, is not

so much *what* is done as *how* it is done. And in this sense, good form in outward demeanor becomes more than a means to an end, more than a subsidiary attribute: it becomes a value in itself, with its own validity and its own effectiveness, and perhaps—human nature being what it is—the greatest value of them all.[75]

Few Americans, even those who call themselves conservatives, would agree. Ronald Steel was right when he pointed out that Kennan was not an *American* conservative.

Kennan is a classic, organic conservative, the intellectual companion of such other historical romanticists as Ortega y Gasset and Spengler. What he deplores is the messiness and leveling of mass democracy, where the median is often the lowest common denominator. What he admires is order, tradition, and an aristocracy of taste and values. Naturally communism is even more abhorrent to him than mass democracy or untrammeled capitalism, for it compounds the sin of leveling by stifling expression.[76]

That is all true. Kennan's was a conservatism of a European kind. "I think your observation that I am intellectually a conservative European shows much penetration," he told George Kateb, an Amherst College political scientist.[77] No doubt his years on the continent help to explain this, though as we have seen, he never professed any faith in democracy, never showed any enthusiasm for indefinite economic growth, and never shared his countrymen's optimism concerning human nature. His disposition and experience of life led him to conclude that it was Hobbes, not Locke (much less Rousseau), who gave us a true picture of the "state of nature."

Before there existed an authority to hold men in check, Hobbes famously asserted, there raged a war of all against all.

Civilization did not, as Rousseau maintained, enslave men; it placed upon them restrictions necessary if a life in common were to be possible. Kennan agreed. When, for example, *New Yorker* writer Nicholas Lemann asked him about the Holocaust, he told him that "it brought home to a great many of us that in a very large proportion of humanity, if some of the cultural restraints and civilizational customs are put to too great a test, there prove to be resources of unmitigated cruelty and evil in most human psyches."[78]

We know that Kennan read Tocqueville, but he never made any systematic study of European conservatism. He read Burke's *Reflections on the Revolution in France* (1790) rather late in life—after, that is, he had already arrived at similar views on his own. There can be no doubt that he agreed with Burke when, in the *Reflections,* the great conservative wrote that he would prefer to suspend his congratulations "on the new liberty of France, until I was informed how it had been combined with government; with public force; with the discipline and obedience of armies; with the collection of an effective and well-distributed revenue; with morality and religion; with the solidity of property; with peace and order; with civil and social manners."[79] Kennan too was loath to praise liberty as an abstract or ideal good; for him, it possessed a value only in a well-ordered society. Left alone, it easily degenerated into license—of the kind that Kennan saw becoming an ever greater threat to America.

Kennan also agreed with Burke's rejection of the notion that tyranny was the only alternative to democracy. "Is it then a truth so universally acknowledged," the Anglo-Irish statesman had asked rhetorically, "that a pure democracy is the only tolerable form into which human society can be thrown, that a man is not permitted to hesitate about its merits, without the suspicion of being a friend to tyranny, that is, of being a foe to mankind?"[80] Kennan believed conservative authoritarianism to be a perfectly legitimate, indeed a better, alternative to either democracy or totalitarianism.

Burke won lasting fame as the most brilliant critic of revolution (of the French kind) and as a persuasive advocate of cautious reform. Kennan was on record as saying that if one wished to change society, "it can be done only as the gardener does it, not as the engineer does it. That is, it's got to be done in harmony with the rules of nature and can't all be done overnight. That's why I'm against practically all revolutions—because they usually end badly by trying to do too much at once."[81]

Kennan always believed that change that was too rapid, even when it was good in itself, had the effect of disrupting the continuity of life, of destroying the individual's confidence in the stability of his world. In a 1960 interview he granted to *Encounter,* he put it this way: "It is my own belief that if you change the lives of people so rapidly that the experience of the father, the wisdom of the father, become irrelevant to the needs of the son, you have done something very dangerous—you have broken the organic bond in the family, and you have created emotional trauma in the minds of young people. That is why I am a conservative."[82]

In the foreword to *Around the Cragged Hill,* Kennan expressed his reluctance to discuss personal and political matters in the abstract and cited Burke: "I cannot [Burke wrote in the *Reflections*] stand forward and give praise or blame to anything which relates to human actions and human concerns on a simple view of the object, as it stands stripped of every relation, in all the nakedness and solitude of metaphysical abstraction. Circumstances . . . give in reality to every political principle its distinguishing color and discriminating effect."[83]

Further on in the same book, Kennan called attention to the passage in Burke's *Letter to the Sheriffs of Bristol* (1777) wherein the illustrious member of the House of Commons patiently explained to his constituents why he had always to vote on the basis of his own best judgment, even if his decision met with their disapproval. To Kennan, that was precisely how representative government was designed to operate—an elite, qualified by education and experience, arriving at decisions not by consulting an ill-informed "people," but through their own disciplined reason.

◆◆◆

We have seen that Kennan was not an American conservative, that he had more in common with conservatives in Europe. But there was one group of Americans whose general outlook he did share: the Southern Agrarians. Perhaps that was because, as John Crowe Ransom, one of the leading Agrarians, put it, "the South is unique on this continent for having founded and defended a culture which was according to the European principles of culture."[84]

Kennan was not, of course, a southerner, and he did not appear to have read the work of Ransom, Allen Tate, Donald Davidson, Robert Penn Warren, or Andrew Nelson Lytle. But he *was* every bit an "agrarian," as hostile to industrialism and to the machine as were they. "I would like," he wrote to a friend in 1964, "to live in an overwhelming agrarian country" where industry was viewed as a "necessary evil." The farmers in the area of Pennsylvania where he had his farm had "many times the self-respect and the spiritual resources of their semi-urban neighbors."[85] Holding such views, he could only have applauded the views advanced in the Agrarians' famous essay collection of 1930, *I'll Take My Stand: The South and the Agrarian Tradition.*

According to the twelve contributors to that manifesto, industry and urban life alienated men and women from the land and from one another, cut them off from nature, taught them that profit was more important than a humane way of life. "A farm is not a place to grow wealthy," Andrew Lytle wrote; "it is a place to grow corn."[86] Like Wendell Berry, who followed in his (and the other Agrarians') footsteps, Lytle regarded industrial farming as a great evil. Kennan, who loved his farm and never thought of it as a means by which to enrich himself, often expressed a similar view. "We stand by," he wrote in *Around the Cragged Hill,* "to witness the rapid decline of family farming and the reckless raiding and ruining of some of the finest agricultural soil on the world's surface, partly by the developers and partly by forms of industrial farming that exploit and exhaust its fertility."[87]

In the brief period during which he served as ambassador to the Soviet Union, Kennan often took advantage of weekends to drive some miles out of Moscow to visit the *dacha* of Associated Press correspondent Thomas P. Whitney and his wife. He loved that rural atmosphere because

> it was a preindustrial life that I was privileged here to observe: a life in which people were doing things with their hands, with animals and with Nature, a life little touched by any form of modernization, a pre–World War I and pre-Revolutionary life, agreeable precisely because it was not a part of, little connected with, in fact disliked and only reluctantly tolerated by, the political establishment of the country in which it existed. How much richer and more satisfying was human existence, after all, when there was not too much of the machine![88]

For Kennan, the family farm was a safe haven from the dehumanizing effects of city life, a place of peace—and above all a place where nature was respected and enjoyed. Consider this lyrical passage from a diary entry, made in December 1953: "Out at the farm the little creek was foaming and gurgling with its minor torrent of muddy water; the sky between the big barn and corn barn was a fiery red. When you walked on the thick winter grass of the lawn you could feel the spongy wetness underneath a faint freezing crust. Above, to the southeast, over the big creek, the first cold winter stars were out, and a sliver of a moon."[89]

The Agrarians were also champions of regionalism—especially, of course, with reference to the South. Let the North live its life and the South live its. But there was something else, the danger of which Tocqueville had warned: the centralization of power. Kennan too believed that the sheer size of America constituted a problem and urged decentralization. The division of the country into some nine republics would, he argued, make for more manageable and effective government. It would also work against the colorless uniformity of habit, of outlook, and of behavior that was obliterating local and sectional differences in ways of life. It was in the name of uniformity and union, Kennan noted late in life, that America inflicted a Civil War upon itself; he believed it would have been better had the South been allowed to go its own way. (It should come as no surprise, then, that he sympathized with the secessionist Second Vermont Republic.)

The Agrarians always had a keen sense of limits, of human weakness, of original sin. This sense is on unforgettable display in Robert Penn Warren's "tale in verse and voices," *Brother to Dragons* (1953). It is the slightly fictionalized story of Thomas Jefferson's nephews, who chopped up a slave and threw the parts of his body into a fire. In Warren's retelling of that chilling event, Jefferson's enlightened belief in human goodness is forever destroyed. When he learned from his nephews' terrible deed, Warren has Jefferson's sister tell him, "what evil was possible even in the familial blood, your fear began, the fear you had always denied, the fear that you—even you—were capable of all."[90]

The Agrarians never shared their countrymen's faith in progress, and while they were in most cases unorthodox in

166

their own beliefs, like Kennan they recognized the contribution Christianity had made to Western civilization. In a strict and nonpejorative sense, they, like him, were reactionaries rather than conservatives. They preferred the past to the present and looked to it for wisdom and guidance.

In a country in which "change" and "progress" are all but worshipped, reactionaries can expect bad press. The United States is a land of futurists, men and women who have convinced themselves that what is to come will always be better than what has been; most Americans lack the Agrarians' tragic sense of life, animated by memory of the Lost Cause. Few retain much memory of the past; for too many of them history, as the student radicals of the 1960s used to say, is "irrelevant." What Donald Davidson, one of the most reactionary of Agrarians, once wrote about Nashville's replica of the Parthenon remains true of modern America: "Pursue not wisdom or virtue here, / But what blind motion, what dim last / Regret of men who slew their past / Raised up this bribe against their fate."

America has its conservatives, but few of them are willing to join Kennan and the Agrarians in articulating such hostility to modernity. They embrace capitalism not merely as the most rational and successful system of economics but as a secular religion; hence they are blind to the system's revolutionary effects and to the vulgarity of its endless appeals to "consumers." For them, economic "growth" has no downside. They believe in democracy and are eager to impose the American system of government on the rest of the world, by force if necessary. They share much of the Left's social agenda, though they prefer to advance it at a slower pace. They believe in science and progress and the essential goodness of man, once freed from ignorance.

It is no accident, then, that Kennan remained a rather lonely figure in American life. He became acutely aware of this when in 1960 someone gave him a subscription to *National Review,* then America's leading, perhaps her only, magazine of conservative opinion. After reading several issues, he penned a letter—never sent—to editor William F. Buckley Jr.; while there was much in its pages with which he could agree, he told Buckley, he could not share the magazine's evident desire to see an all-out war with Soviet Russia or its sympathy for Senator Joseph McCarthy. Perhaps most tellingly, he mentioned that he had known European correspondent Erik von Kuehnelt-Leddihn "as a kindred spirit in political philosophy long before the *National Review* was established."[91]

Although he served for brief periods on the faculties at Georgetown, Fordham, and Chestnut Hill, Kuehnelt-Leddihn was born in Austria and earned his doctorate in Budapest; he never felt at home in the United States and, as soon as possible, returned to Europe. A relentless critic of democracy, he argued that it easily transformed itself, with a logic both consistent and murderous, into socialism—international and national. Contrary to received opinion, Kuehnelt-Leddihn regarded these revolutionary movements as rivals rather than enemies, brothers under the skin.

Kennan did have a good bit in common with the Michigan-based traditionalist Russell Kirk, but he did not seem to be aware of the fact. He was most pleased, therefore, to find in the Hungarian-born John Lukacs, who replaced Kuehnelt-Leddihn at Chestnut Hill College, another kindred spirit. Like Kennan, Lukacs takes a dim view of what passes for American conservatism—its cults of science and progress, its religion of democracy, its belief that only other peoples are sinful. Lukacs prefers to identify himself as a reactionary, someone who *resists* much of modernity and loves the past. In his splendid *Confessions of an Original Sinner* (1990), he wrote that he "loved and admired and longed for the better things of the past, especially of a past whose presence I could still see and hear and smell and sense, physically and mentally."[92] Lukacs's *George Kennan:*

*A Study of Character* (2007) is at once a fine portrait of its subject and a moving tribute to a friend. If America can be said to have a reactionary tradition, the friends Kennan and Lukacs surely have been two of its leading representatives.

# Conclusion: "Mistress"

During the brief time that he served as ambassador to the USSR, Kennan visited Yasnaya Polyana, Tolstoy's estate. While strolling through the grounds with Valentin Bulgakov, Tolstoy's last private secretary, he felt "close to a world to which, I always thought, I could really have belonged, had circumstances permitted—belonged much more naturally and wholeheartedly than to the world of politics and diplomacy into which Fate had thrust me."[1] To borrow from Chekhov, diplomacy was his wife, but writing was his mistress.

Kennan served *in* the world of diplomatic affairs for many years, but he was never *of* it. Consider, for example, some reflective words in his introduction to *The Fateful Alliance,* a study, as we have seen, of the diplomatic negotiations leading to the pivotal Franco-Russian alliance of 1894. The reader should remember, he wrote, that Paris and St. Petersburg, the scenes of most of the negotiations, were then experiencing a richness of literary and artistic activity—"an outpouring beside which the written records of the dealings among statesmen . . . appear obscure, colorless, and dreary, like dust-covered legal documents."[2]

Paris, he pointed out, was witnessing an almost unparalleled flowering of the visual arts, and although literature had not reached similar heights, Zola and Maurice Barrès were in their prime, and other writers—Claudel, Proust, Anatole France—were waiting in the wings. In the world of music, Camille Saint-Saëns was at the peak of his popularity, while works by Russian composers—Rimski-Korsakov, Tchaikovsky, Moussorgsky, Borodin—attracted large and enthusiastic audiences. The same composers contributed to a Russian culture on the threshold of one of its greatest eras. While it could always boast of its religious art—its iconography—it now began to produce secular artists of European stature. And then there were the Russian writers; Tolstoy was still at work, and Chekhov was about to give the theater the great plays of the 1895–1904 period.

Were the statesmen about whom Kennan was to write aware of this cultural ferment? Based upon his own experience, he did not see how they could remain oblivious. And yet they were busy men, burdened with serious responsibilities. Kennan concluded his reflections with these personally revealing words:

> The responsibilities were important ones; and someone had to bear them. So they struggled along . . . in another world from that of the artists, the writers, and the musicians. It was their professional world—a world of duty. And if they were moved, or disturbed, by the cultural frenzy of the time, there was nothing they could do about it. All that was their private life. They were obliged to keep it aloof from their official duties.[3]

That this was a poignant meditation upon his own diplomatic career can hardly be doubted. We know how he took advantage of every opportunity to write in his diaries, pursue his study of Chekhov, read German and French novels, and attend concerts. In a diary entry of November 28, 1927—he was then in Hamburg—he tells of being present at a concert given by Vladimir Horowitz, whose greatness and nervous constitution he recognized immediately. A professional critic would have had difficulty improving upon his account of the performance. "When he played (it was a Tchaikovski concerto) it seemed as though he himself were being played upon by some unseen musician—as though every note were being wrung out of him. His nervous, spidery fingers trembled on the keys, his face worked as though he were in agony, perspiration dripped from his forehead, and he groaned with every chord of the crescendo passages."[4]

From his earliest years Kennan's true interests were cultural and literary. Almost from the beginning he was, before anything else, a writer—one who aspired to literary distinction. It was primarily because he had had to refine his prose style while composing diplomatic papers that he concluded that historical writing was the only realistic avenue open to him when he joined the Institute for Advanced Study's School of Historical Studies; the institute does not offer membership to creative writers. (Director Frank Aydelotte made an exception when, in November 1946, he invited T. S. Eliot to come to the institute as a visiting member of the School of Historical Studies and as the first unofficial artist-in-residence. Eliot arrived in October 1948 but had to leave the following month in order to travel to Sweden to accept the Nobel Prize in Literature.)

History it would have to be, but like Veronica (C. V.) Wedgwood, whom he knew and admired, Kennan regarded historical writing as a branch of literature—both Winston Churchill and Theodor Mommsen, he once pointed out, had won the Nobel Prize in *Literature*. "The literary historian," he told a New York gathering of the PEN club in 1959, "writes prose, and it seems to me very much the same kind that the strictly literary person does."[5] Anyone who had read his first historical study, *Russia Leaves the War* (1956), would have had to agree. In the first paragraph of a beautifully written prologue, he described what was then Petrograd in this way: "Cleaving the city down the center, the cold waters of the Neva move silently and swiftly, like a slab of smooth grey metal, past the granite embankments and the ponderous palaces, bringing with them the tang of the lonely wastes of forests and swamp from which they have emerged. At every hand one feels the proximity of the great wilderness of the Russian north—silent, sombre, infinitely patient."[6]

His habit of making sketches contributed much to Kennan's rare ability to describe city and rural landscapes (it is no accident that he titled his diary selections *Sketches from a Life*). But he also possessed a talent for the verbal sketching of personalities. He devoted a fascinating chapter of *Russia Leaves the War* to Woodrow Wilson, Robert Lansing, Lenin, Trotsky, Raymond Robins, and John Reed. For Reed, the author of the pro-Bolshevik *Ten Days That Shook the World* (1919), Kennan had surprisingly kind words, for he saw in him "a poet of the first order." Despite its communist outlook, Reed's history of the revolution stood above every other contemporary account "for its literary power, its penetration, its command of detail."[7] For those who possessed literary gifts, Kennan always felt the greatest admiration.

He himself had a gift. In addition to the National Book Award, the Pulitzer Prize, and the Bancroft Prize, *Russia Leaves the War* won the Benjamin Franklin Award for the best work of history as literature—no doubt the award that meant the most to Kennan. But it was not just award committees; no one who has written about Kennan has failed to call attention to the literary style that he perfected. It was old-fashioned in the best sense of that much-abused word—formal, graceful, unhurried; Gibbonesque.

In Kennan's view, the historian and creative writer both strove for beauty in the use of language. Moreover, they shared a desire to uncover truth, understood as something more than factual accuracy. "Tolkien has given us, in *The Fellowship of the Ring,* a work of pure fantasy, dealing even with an imagined world and with a people other than human," he remarked, "and yet it is impregnated at every turn with truth." Because serious fiction viewed truth as understanding, Kennan was always tempted to move from what was reliably known to have been "to the more exciting and colourful world of what might very well have been and probably was."[8]

On the last page of *The Decision to Intervene* (1958), for example, he described the departure from Soviet territory of two American members of the Red Cross Mission. The description included mention of "a tethered nanny goat" nibbling "patiently at the sparse dying foliage."[9] He later confessed that he could not document the presence of the goat, but that he could not recall such a scene in Russia without one; a good historian, C. V. Wedgwood once observed, should be able to draw upon his own experience to illuminate that of others.[10]

When describing the funeral of Nikolai Giers in *The Fateful Alliance,* Kennan again went beyond what he could prove. The date was January 31, 1895, the place a monastery on the shores of the Gulf of Finland. It was, Kennan knew—because he had gone to the trouble of checking the contemporary weather report in the St. Petersburg newspapers—a cold and wintry day. But he did not know for certain that "a chill wind swept in from across the partially frozen waters of the gulf."[11] Most likely it did, and saying so made for a paragraph that, because it read so convincingly and well, offered readers a truer vision of the past.

When working on his family history, Kennan found even more room for his creative imagination, because the data available was so limited. "I have," he stated in his preface, "taken account here not only of such events as appeared *provable* by documentary evidence, but also of such others as seemed sufficiently *probable* to deserve mention."[12] This, of course, is a dangerous game, but when played by a historian of Kennan's caliber and integrity, it can help to transform mere chronology into compelling narrative history, the literary character of which appealed to Kennan as a writer.

Good narrative history reads like a novel and sometimes moves—with due caution—beyond what can be verified by documents. In recent years there have been many attempts to write what might be described as novelized histories that take history as the subject and not merely as the background, as it is in historical novels. John Dos Passos, Irwin Shaw, Gore Vidal, E. L. Doctorow, Don DeLillo, and Jeff Shaara have all contributed to this emerging genre. And so has a much finer writer, Aleksandr Solzhenitsyn, whose *Red Wheel* (1971–91) is a novelized history of Russia during the Great War. In *Lenin in Zurich* (1976), published separately, Solzhenitsyn put words in the Bolshevik leader's mouth consistent with his manner of speaking, as reported by those who knew him at the time—and in that way he gave us as true a portrait of the tyrant as we are likely ever to get.

John Lukacs has made a still bolder attempt to write a new kind of history, the kind "when the writer knows, in the marrow of his bones, not only that France in 1789 became different from France in 1788, but how, say, Paris in 1905 differed from Paris in 1902."[13] In a brilliant performance titled *A Thread of Years* (1998), he offered readers a series of "vignettes," fictional *petits faits* that clearly *did* not but *could* have occurred in particular places in particular years, beginning in 1901 and ending in 1969. In them he hoped readers would see reflected the larger movements of history.

But even with greater leeway, Kennan believed, the historian could not reach into "the inner world" of his subjects. He could speak with authority only of their external personalities as revealed by their words and actions. The creative writer, on the other hand, could cast light on "the anarchy, the tenderness, and the brutality of the individual soul"; he was after "truth of a deeper and more intimate nature. It is primarily truth sensed, felt, and molded for effect, only secondarily truth observed."[14] The historian could indeed increase self-knowledge by recording what other men—men, after all, like himself—had said and done, but only the novelist or poet could make possible the kind of intimate, profoundly personal self-understanding that was one of the chief goals of all of Kennan's writing.

In his history of Russian-American relations from 1917 to 1920, Kennan once declared, he had been "concerned with what can be proven to have occurred to men in the broader aspects of their political and social dealings with one another. [In *Dr. Zhivago*] Pasternak was concerned to reveal, out of the workings of the artist's sensitivity and intuition, as well as out of his own memories, the sort of thing that could and did happen to individuals in their intimate reactions to these events. His was a vastly greater contribution than mine."[15] He had in mind the attempts by Yuri Zhivago and Lara to live a quiet private life during the tumultuous years of the Great War, the Russian Revolutions, and the Russian Civil War.

With the exception of brief periods of escape to a remote village, the lovers never find peace in a broken world. Through their experiences, Pasternak was able to help his readers to understand the human cost of great historic upheavals—and Kennan stood in awe of his achievement. No doubt he had the Russian writer in mind when, in a piece for the *New York Times Book Review,* he wrote: "It is with the intimate undercurrent of men's lives that the true literary artist is permitted to deal, and does deal, in his greatest moments—with the inner souls of men rather than with what Freud has called their personae"[16]—with Yuri the sensitive poet, not Dr. Zhivago the skilled physician.

"Of those of us who try to write history as literature," Kennan confessed, "there are few, I am sure, who do not sometimes peek longingly through the curtain into that more mysterious and more exciting and more dangerous world in which others are privileged to operate."[17] For that reason, his diaries meant more to him than his histories or political writings—it was in them that he was able to peek through the curtain at himself, to come to know himself as a person and not just as a persona, a public figure.

His diary entries are windows into his soul; it is a pity that he published only a small selection of them. He did, however, publish two volumes of memoirs, and they represent his finest published literary achievement. We know that he regarded them as literature because of what he wrote in the late 1950s: "It is an interesting reflection on the relationship of history to literature . . . that whereas biography is history, autobiography is literature."[18]

To be sure, his autobiographical writings concerned his career in the foreign service, but in accepting a National Book Award for his first volume of memoirs, Kennan spoke of a connection between professional diplomacy and literature:

> Professional diplomacy came into being in what might be called the dynastic period of European history. . . . This was an age when kings were expected to speak well, and often did; and diplomacy, saddled with the duty of speaking in their name, was expected to speak the same way. . . . It endeavored to embody the dignity, the serenity, the ceremoniousness and the elegance to which the royal court was committed. It was a highly mannered language, decorous and studiedly courteous. It attempted to draw a curtain over the baser nature of the writer. . . . [It] was a part of man's effort to become, if only by pretending to be, something more than his pathetic disreputable self; and often it succeeded.[19]

That statement was confessional. It revealed the fact that Kennan thought of his writing, even his diplomatic papers, as literary in character. It shows too the importance he attributed to beauty of expression—like all creations of beauty, good writing was religious in inspiration; it lifted both the writer and his readers above their animal origins, making of them something more and better than they would otherwise have been. In that way it helped to preserve civilization, for Kennan agreed with what Ortega y Gasset wrote three years before Nazi barbarism engulfed Germany: "Civilization is *not* always with us. It is not self-sustaining. Civilization is artificial and requires an artist or an artisan. If you want the fruits of civilization but do not care to cultivate and nurture it—you are fooling yourself. In a trice, you can be left without civilization."[20]

In the late 1960s, Kennan had reason to remind his fellow writers and artists of that stubborn fact. He repeatedly protested the politicization of cultural life and, in his opening address as president of the American Academy of Arts and Letters, he stated his conviction "that the vicissitudes of war and politics should never be permitted to interfere with the work of the creative artist," whose duty it was to lend to the comprehension of the human predicament a deeper dimension of insight. His work should not be set aside "because somewhere the guns are speaking, or because there is brawling in the streets." He cited as those who had remained faithful to their calling during times of war Goethe and Schiller and Jean Sibelius. "And most eloquent and timely of all, to my mind, is the image of Pasternak's Zhivago, who was of course Pasternak himself, scratching out his poems through the night in that abandoned country house in the Urals during the Russian civil war."[21]

✦✦✦

Kennan's memoirs, particularly the first volume, are built around entries from his diaries; they testify to their author's "tragic sense of life," a sense analyzed with insight by the Spanish philosopher Miguel de Unamuno. All of us, Unamuno taught in *Del sentimiento trágico de la vida* (1913), long for immortality; we cannot tolerate the thought of nonbeing, of annihilation. Moreover, we want desperately to know our destination—where it is that we are headed. Some find reassurance and comfort in religious faith, though even the most devout experience periods of doubt. Since the Renaissance and the scientific revolution, many have despaired because their reason teaches them that there is no personal immortality. Yet even atheists, whatever they may say, secretly resist this conclusion. A conflict rages within all of us between what the world is as reason shows it to be and what we wish it might be, what our faith (however denied or hidden) affirms it to be. Our awareness of that conflict is, according to Unamuno, the tragic sense of life.

Kennan experienced conflicts of a similar kind—between his rational approach to diplomacy and his spiritual (in the broad sense) approach to life, between his deist belief in the Primary Cause and his more orthodox belief in the Merciful Deity, between the pull of animality and the desire for civilization. Concerning the latter, as we have seen, he found psychoanalysis to be instructive. To that philosophy, as he regarded it, he was introduced by William Bullitt, who knew Freud well and collaborated with him on a psychological study of Woodrow Wilson—a devastating examination that was published only in 1966.

While convalescing in Vienna in 1935, Kennan read Freud's *Vorlesungen zur Einführung in die Psychoanalyse* (*Introductory Lectures on Psycho-Analysis*, published in English in 1933) and was immediately struck by it. Later, we know, he read *Das Unbehagen in der Kultur*. Those books and others from Freud's pen offered him an explanation for the tragic sense that seems to have been his from youth. From the founder of psychoanalysis, he learned that humans are fundamentally instinctual rather than rational beings, and that the price of civilization is instinctual repression—with its attendant discontent.

In Belgrade, Kennan delivered a sermon on Freud and Calvin in which he emphasized their common recognition of the darker side of human nature. His words on that occasion show that he found in Freud's work scientific confirmation of the doctrine of original sin. That doctrine leads to the tragic conclusion that while sin can be brought under control—and more important, forgiven—it can never, or only very rarely, be completely overcome. Kennan told Nicholas Lemann that he was drawn to Christianity precisely "because it recognizes in the human condition the same element of tragedy that I recognize myself." Few humans were able to attain perfection. "Damn few: the saints. The rest are caught between innate good qualities and wholly uncontrollable—animalistic if you will—instinctive compulsions that come to bear."[22]

Kennan often called attention to life's quotidian tragedies—the death of family members and friends, crippling accidents and diseases, the diminishing powers that accompany advancing age, consciousness of mortality. Over these, men and women exercise little or no control, but they all contribute to human suffering. Kennan was particularly irked by those radical students who evidenced "no appreciation for the element of tragedy that unavoidably constitutes a central component of man's predicament and no understanding for the resulting limitations on the possibilities for social and political achievement."[23]

This tragic sense makes itself felt throughout Kennan's diaries and memoirs. In Berlin, early in 1931, he wrote of "the droning of a lonely trolley car, whining hopelessly, sleepily, through the night, from an unknown origin to an unknown destination"[24]—rather like human beings, he undoubtedly thought to himself. Late in 1939, in the same city, he recorded a long conversation with a prostitute—over drinks in a neighborhood bar. He intended to dramatize the fact that the Germans were not all monsters who supported Hitler's war; neither she nor he so much as mentioned the conflict then raging. What strikes the reader even more forcefully, however, is the woman's tragic existence—her degrading profession, her loneliness, her inability to break free of an abusive lover.

Kennan's tragic sense of life was a result of his profound sensitivity not merely to human imperfection, but to human imperfectibility, including his own. He came to think that he had not been critical enough of his own life and conduct—that his was finally a failure of self-knowledge, of full recognition of his personal responsibility for his failures and shortcomings. His memoirs speak repeatedly, almost obsessively, of those supposed failures and shortcomings, both personal and professional.

In this regard, however, he had absorbed too much of his Calvinist heritage. He was a man of exemplary character who was honest and forthright in dealings with others and generous in his judgment of those with whom he had serious disagreements, even of those who had treated him unjustly. Two of his institute secretaries, Liz Stenard and Terri Bramley, remember that he treated everyone, of whatever station in life, with respect.[25]

It is true that his professional warnings concerning the dangers of "immoderate greatness" were generally ignored, but as a result the United States has paid a steep price. Nor was his service to his country limited to the field of foreign policy. He cautioned repeatedly that a lack of self-discipline and an uncritical egalitarianism were leading America and the West down the road to ruin; that few were willing to listen was no fault of his.

A prophet without honor, he left behind a body of written work that will continue to be read, not only as history, but as literature; indeed, his memoirs were recognized as literary classics on publication. So inspired is the prose that he perfected that those who write about him quickly discover that they must rely upon extensive quotation. "In Kennan's writings," John Lukacs has observed, "there are passages so well written, so illuminating, that [commentators] can hardly paraphrase or improve on them, or not at all."[26] He was, in a word, a true artist. Measured by his literary distinction, service to country, wisdom, and character, George Kennan was the greatest American of the century now ended.

# Notes

## One: The Foreign Service

1. George F. Kennan, *An American Family: The Kennans—The First Three Generations* (New York: W. W. Norton, 2000), 23.
2. Ibid., 128–29.
3. George F. Kennan, *Memoirs, 1925–1950* (Boston: Little, Brown, 1967), 4.
4. George F. Kennan, *Sketches from a Life* (New York: Pantheon Books, 1989), 165.
5. George F. Kennan, "The Value of a St. John's Education," in *Speeches of Significance Climaxing the 75th Anniversary Commencement* (Delafield, WI: St. John's Military Academy, 1960), 6.
6. Cited in Don Oberdorfer, *Princeton University: The First 250 Years* (Princeton, NJ: Princeton University, 1995), 122.
7. F. Scott Fitzgerald, *This Side of Paradise* (New York: Charles Scribner's Sons, 1920), 33.
8. George F. Kennan, *Around the Cragged Hill: A Personal and Political Philosophy* (New York: W. W. Norton, 1993), 23.
9. George F. Kennan, *American Diplomacy, 1900–1950* (New York: Mentor Books, 1951), 80.
10. Kennan, *Memoirs, 1925–1950,* 21.
11. Kennan, *Sketches from a Life,* x.
12. George Kennan, *Siberia and the Exile System,* introduced by George Frost Kennan (Chicago: University of Chicago Press, 1958 [1891]), 115.
13. Ibid., 63.
14. George Frost Kennan, introduction to ibid., xviii.
15. Kennan, *Sketches from a Life,* 16.

16. Kennan, *Memoirs, 1925–1950,* 34, 37.
17. Ibid., 47.
18. George F. Kennan, "Memorandum for the Minister," *New York Review of Books,* April 26, 2001, 23.
19. Quoted in Ronald Hingley, *Chekhov: A Biographical and Critical Study* (London: George Allen and Unwin, 1950), 115.
20. Kennan, *Memoirs, 1925–1950,* 49.
21. George F. Kennan, lecture ("The Revolutionary Movement"), Princeton University, February 26, 1964, George F. Kennan Papers, box 21, folder 14, Public Policy Papers, Department of Rare Books and Special Collections, Princeton University Library.
22. Kennan, *Memoirs, 1925–1950,* 53.
23. George F. Kennan, introduction to Orville H. Bullitt, ed., *For the President: Personal and Secret: Correspondence Between Franklin D. Roosevelt and William C. Bullitt* (Boston: Houghton Mifflin, 1972), xv-xvi.
24. Kennan, *Memoirs, 1925–1950,* 57.
25. Quoted in David Mayers, *George Kennan and the Dilemmas of US Foreign Policy* (New York: Oxford University Press, 1988), 44.
26. Quoted in Robert Conquest, *The Great Terror: A Reassessment* (New York: Oxford University Press, 1990), 164.
27. George F. Kennan, "Interview for CNN Cold War Series," September 27, 1998, http://www.gwu.edu/~nsarchiv/coldwar/interviews/episode-1/Kennan3.html. Accessed August 20, 2006.
28. George F. Kennan, Fair Day, Adieu!, 1938, George F. Kennan Papers, box 25, p. 56.
29. Kennan, *Sketches from a Life,* 43.
30. Kennan, *Memoirs, 1925–1950,* 77.
31. Quoted in Mayers, *George Kennan and the Dilemmas of US Foreign Policy,* 50–51.
32. Quoted in ibid., 53.
33. Quoted in ibid., 54.
34. Paul Schmidt to the author and other American GIs, Bad Aibling, West Germany, sometime in 1964.
35. Kennan, *Memoirs, 1925–1950,* 93.
36. Quoted in Mayers, *George Kennan and the Dilemmas of US Foreign Policy,* 68.
37. George F. Kennan, *From Prague after Munich: Diplomatic Papers, 1938–1940* (Princeton, NJ: Princeton University Press, 1968), 5.
38. Ibid.
39. Quoted in Joseph Epstein, "The Author as Character," *Weekly Standard* 9, no. 45 (2004): 34.
40. Quoted in John Lukacs, *George Kennan: A Study of Character* (New Haven, CT: Yale University Press, 2007), 50n.

41. Kennan, *Sketches from a Life*, 47.
42. Ibid.
43. Agostino von Hassell and Sigrid MacRae (with Simone Ameskamp), *Alliance of Enemies: The Untold Story of the Secret American and German Collaboration to End World War II* (New York: St. Martin's Press, 2006), 229.
44. Quoted in ibid., 304.
45. George F. Kennan, "Noble Man," *New York Review of Books* 20, no. 4 (1973), http://www.nybooks.com/articles/9906. Accessed August 24, 2006.
46. Joachim Fest, *Plotting Hitler's Death: The Story of the German Resistance*, trans. Bruce Little (New York: Henry Holt, 1996), 159.
47. Letter, George F. Kennan to G. van Roon, March 14, 1962, George F. Kennan Papers, box 31, folder 8.
48. Kennan, *Memoirs, 1925–1950*, 122.
49. Ibid., 119.
50. Quoted in ibid., 130.
51. Ibid., 136.
52. Charles B. Burdick, *An American Island in Hitler's Reich: The Bad Nauheim Internment* (Menlo Park, CA: Markgraf Publications Group, 1987), 63.
53. George F. Kennan, lecture on Russian History, Bad Nauheim, 1942, George F. Kennan Papers, box 16, folder 4, p. 17.
54. George F. Kennan, lecture on Russian History, Bad Nauheim, 1942, George F. Kennan Papers, box 16, folder 6, pp. 1–4.
55. Kennan, *Memoirs, 1925–1950*, 137.
56. Quoted in Mayers, *George Kennan and the Dilemmas of US Foreign Policy*, 343n.
57. Kennan, *Memoirs, 1925–1950*, 179.
58. George F. Kennan, remarks to officer staff of the Legation at Lisbon, June 1944, George F. Kennan Papers, box 16, folder 9, p. 10.
59. Kennan, *Memoirs, 1925–1950*, 184–85.
60. Ibid., 218.
61. Ibid., 225.
62. Ibid., 512.
63. Ibid., 531.
64. Ibid., 230–31, 233.
65. Ibid., 534.
66. Ibid., 272.
67. Kennan, *Sketches from a Life*, 107–9.
68. Kennan, *Memoirs, 1925–1950*, 293.
69. Ibid.
70. Ibid., 554.

71. Harvey Klehr, John Earl Haynes, and Fridrikh Igorevich Firsov, *The Secret World of American Communism* (New Haven, CT: Yale University Press, 1995), 326.
72. Kennan, *Memoirs, 1925–1950,* 554.
73. Klehr, Haynes, and Firsov, *The Secret World,* 323.
74. Kennan, *Memoirs, 1925–1950,* 294–95.
75. Letter, George F. Kennan to John Osborne, July 31, 1962, George F. Kennan Papers, box 31, folder 8.
76. Kennan, *Memoirs, 1925–1950,* 307.
77. Giles D. Harlow and George C. Maerz, introduction to George F. Kennan, *Measures Short of War: The George F. Kennan Lectures at the National War College, 1946–47,* ed. by Giles D. Harlow and George C. Maerz (Washington, DC: National Defense University Press, 1991), xxvii.
78. George F. Kennan, ibid., 289.
79. Ibid., 13.
80. Ibid., 14.
81. Kennan, *Memoirs, 1925–1950,* 310.
82. Edward Gibbon, *The Decline and Fall of the Roman Empire,* vol. I (New York: The Modern Library, n.d.), 291.
83. George F. Kennan, "The Sources of Soviet Conduct" in *American Diplomacy, 1900–1950,* 93.
84. Quoted in ibid., 90–91.
85. Ibid., 98–99.
86. Ibid., 103–4.
87. Kennan, *Measures Short of War,* 210.
88. Quoted in Wilson D. Miscamble, *George F. Kennan and the Making of American Foreign Policy, 1947–1950* (Princeton, NJ: Princeton University Press, 1992), 89.
89. Kennan, *Memoirs, 1925–1950,* 322–23.
90. Walter Lippmann, *The Cold War: A Study in U.S. Foreign Policy* (New York: Harper and Brothers, 1947), 44.
91. "Policy Planning Staff/1: Policy with Respect to American Aid to Western Europe," *Foreign Relations of the United States,* III (1947): 223–30.
92. Ibid.
93. George C. Marshall, "The Marshall Plan Speech," http://www.georgecmarshall.org/1t/speeches/marshall_plan.cfm. Accessed August 21, 2006.
94. "PPS Memorandum: Inauguration of Organized Political Warfare," May 4, 1948, http://academic.brooklyn.cuny.edu/history/johnson/65ciafounding3.htm. Accessed August 23, 2006.
95. Quoted in Miscamble, *George F. Kennan and the Making of American Foreign Policy, 109.*

96. George F. Kennan, "Spy and Counterspy," *New York Times,* May 18, 1997.

97. Ibid.

98. Quoted in Peter Coleman, *The Liberal Conspiracy: The Congress for Cultural Freedom and the Struggle for the Mind of Postwar Europe* (New York: The Free Press, 1989), 234.

99. George F. Kennan, "The Challenge of Freedom," *New Leader* 38, no. 51 (1955): 12.

100. George F. Kennan, paper prepared for International Seminar on Industrial Society, Basle, Switzerland, September 20–26, 1959, George F. Kennan Papers, box 26, folder 1-E-19.

101. Kennan, *Memoirs, 1925–1950,* 415.

102. Quoted in Walter Isaacson and Evan Thomas, *The Wise Men: Six Friends and the World They Made* (New York: Touchstone, 1988), 290.

103. Quoted in A. C. Grayling, *Among the Dead Cities: The History and Moral Legacy of the WW II Bombing of Civilians in Germany and Japan* (New York: Walker and Company, 2006), 83.

104. Kennan, *Sketches from a Life,* 121.

105. Paul Johnson, *Modern Times: The World from the Twenties to the Nineties* (New York: Harper Perennial, 1991), 370.

106. Grayling, *Among the Dead Cities,* 168.

107. Kennan, *Around the Cragged Hill,* 220.

108. Quoted in Miscamble, *George F. Kennan and the Making of American Foreign Policy,* 181.

109. See James Burnham, *Containment or Liberation? An Inquiry into the Aims of United States Foreign Policy* (New York: John Day, 1953).

110. Letter, George F. Kennan to "Tom," April 12, 1956, George F. Kennan Papers, box 31, folder 2.

111. Kennan, *Memoirs, 1925–1950,* 495.

112. George F. Kennan, "Report on Latin America," *Foreign Relations of the United States,* 1950, II, 598–624.

113. Kennan, *Sketches from a Life,* 130–31.

114. Institute for Advanced Study, *Annual Report for the Fiscal Year July 1, 1981–June 30, 1982* (Princeton, NJ: The Institute for Advanced Study, 1982), 11.

115. Abraham Flexner, quoted in *The Institute Letter,* Institute for Advanced Study, Winter 2007, p. 1.

116. George F. Kennan in ibid., back page.

117. George F. Kennan, *Memoirs, 1950–1963* (Boston: Little, Brown, 1972), 14.

118. Ibid., 5.

119. Kennan, *Sketches from a Life,* 143.

120. Kennan, *American Diplomacy,* 83.

121. Ibid., 87.
122. Ibid., 49.
123. Kennan, *Memoirs, 1950–1963,* 82.
124. Kennan, *Sketches from a Life,* 145.
125. Letter, George F. Kennan to Lewis Douglas, August 12, 1952, George F. Kennan Papers, box 29, folder 5.
126. Letter, George F. Kennan to The President, August 11, 1952, George F. Kennan Papers, box 29, folder 4.
127. Kennan, *Memoirs, 1950–1963,* 159.
128. Letter, George F. Kennan to Bernard Gufler, October 27, 1952, George F. Kennan Papers, box 29, folder 5.
129. Letter, George F. Kennan to Louis J. Halle, April 20, 1966, George F. Kennan Papers, box 31, folder 12.

## Two: The Institute for Advanced Study

1. Kennan, *Sketches from a Life,* 174.
2. George F. Kennan, *Russia, the Atom, and the West: The BBC Reith Lectures, 1957* (London: Oxford University Press, 1958), 26.
3. Ibid., 13.
4. Ibid., 101.
5. Quoted in Kennan, *Memoirs, 1950–1963,* 236.
6. Letter, Michael Polanyi to George F. Kennan, November 11, 1957, George F. Kennan Papers, box 30, folder 2-A.
7. Kennan, *Memoirs, 1950–1963,* 261.
8. Lukacs, *George Kennan,* 156.
9. George F. Kennan, *Russia and the West Under Lenin and Stalin* (New York: Mentor, 1961), 50.
10. Ibid., 15.
11. Ibid., 229.
12. Dmitri Volkogonov, *Lenin: A New Biography,* trans. and ed. Harold Shukman (New York: Free Press, 1994), 235.
13. All quoted in Richard Pipes, ed., *The Unknown Lenin: From the Secret Archive,* with the assistance of David Brandenberger, trans. Catherine A. Fitzpatrick (New Haven, CT: Yale University Press, 1996), 11, 50, 152–55.
14. Kennan, *Russia and the West Under Lenin and Stalin,* 314.
15. Ibid., 239.
16. Ibid., 142, 180.
17. Ibid., 344.
18. Ibid., 366.
19. Ibid., 371.

20. George F. Kennan, Reflections, January 1959, George F. Kennan Papers, box 26, folder 1-E-17.
21. George F. Kennan, *Soviet-American Relations, 1917–1920, I: Russia Leaves the War* (Princeton, NJ: Princeton University Press, 1956), vii.
22. Letter, George F. Kennan to Herbert Butterfield, December 17, 1956, George F. Kennan Papers, box 31, folder 2.
23. Kennan, *Soviet-American Relations, I: Russia Leaves the War,* 12.
24. Ibid., 82.
25. William C. Bullitt, "The Size of a Banana," *National Review* 2, no. 29 (1956): 14.
26. Quoted in Kennan, *Soviet-American Relations, I: Russia Leaves the War,* 422.
27. George F. Kennan, *Soviet-American Relations, 1917–1920, II: The Decision to Intervene* (Princeton, NJ: Princeton University Press, 1958), v.
28. Pipes, ed., *The Unknown Lenin,* 42–46.
29. Quoted in Kennan, *Soviet-American Relations, II: The Decision to Intervene,* 152.
30. Ibid., 7.
31. Ibid., 13.
32. Ibid.
33. George F. Kennan, *At a Century's Ending: Reflections, 1982–1995* (New York: W. W. Norton, 1996), 303–4.
34. Kennan, *Soviet-American Relations, II: The Decision to Intervene,* 329.
35. Kennan, *Sketches from a Life,* 178.
36. Ibid., 183.
37. Ibid., 194–95.
38. Quoted in Associated Press, "Yugoslavs Ponder Kennan's Role," *Christian Science Monitor,* July 18, 1961.
39. Letter, George F. Kennan to J. Robert Oppenheimer, November 16, 1962, George F. Kennan Papers, box 31, folder 8.
40. Letter, George F. Kennan to Josip Broz Tito, December 12, 1963, George F. Kennan Papers, box 31, folder 9.
41. George F. Kennan, unused material for second volume of memoirs, 1970, George F. Kennan Papers, box 27, folder 1-E-28.
42. George F. Kennan, *Democracy and the Student Left* (New York: Bantam Books, 1968), 192.
43. Ibid., 8–9.
44. All quoted in ibid., 39, 65–66, 78.
45. Ibid., 131, 134, 189.
46. George F. Kennan, "Introducing Eugene McCarthy," *New York Review of Books* 10, no. 7 (1968), http://www.nybooks.com/articles/11729. Accessed August 25, 2006.
47. Kennan, *Democracy and the Student Left,* 148–49.

48. George F. Kennan, "On 'Speak Truth to Power,'" *Progressive,* October 1955, 18.
49. Kennan, *Democracy and the Student Left,* 150.
50. George F. Kennan, *Decline of the West? George Kennan and His Critics,* ed. Martin F. Herz (Washington, DC: Ethics and Public Policy Center, 1978), 8–9.
51. Quoted in George F. Kennan, *The Marquis de Custine and His Russia in 1839* (Princeton, NJ: Princeton University Press, 1971), 92.
52. Kennan, *Democracy and the Student Left,* 204.
53. Kennan, *The Marquis de Custine,* 130–31.
54. George F. Kennan, *The Decline of Bismarck's European Order: Franco-Russian Relations, 1875–1890* (Princeton, NJ: Princeton University Press, 1979), 3–4.
55. Ibid., 27–28.
56. Quoted in William L. Langer, *The Franco-Russian Alliance, 1890–1894* (New York: Octagon Books, 1977 [1929]), 106.
57. Kennan, *The Decline of Bismarck's European Order,* 365.
58. Ibid., 373.
59. Ibid., 368.
60. Kennan, *At a Century's Ending,* 308.
61. George F. Kennan, *The Fateful Alliance: France, Russia, and the Coming of the First World War* (New York: Pantheon Books, 1984), 235.
62. For a good discussion of Clausewitz, see Michael Howard, *Clausewitz* (Oxford: Oxford University Press, 1983).
63. Kennan, *The Fateful Alliance,* 164, 257.
64. George F. Kennan, *The Nuclear Delusion: Soviet-American Relations in the Atomic Age* (New York: Pantheon Books, 1983), 147.
65. Kennan, *At a Century's Ending,* 70.
66. Kai Bird and Martin J. Sherwin, *American Prometheus: The Triumph and Tragedy of J. Robert Oppenheimer* (New York: Alfred A. Knopf, 2005), 4.
67. Kennan, *Memoirs, 1950–1963,* 20.
68. Edward Teller, *Memoirs: A Twentieth-Century Journey in Science and Politics,* with Judith Shoolery (Cambridge, MA: Perseus, 2001), 572.
69. Jerrold and Leona Schecter, *Sacred Secrets: How Soviet Intelligence Operations Changed American History* (Washington, DC: Brassey's, 2002), 49–51, 56.
70. Oppenheimer's testimony in Teller, *Memoirs,* 376.
71. Quoted in Bird and Sherwin, *American Prometheus,* 526.
72. George F. Kennan, "In Defense of Oppenheimer," *New York Review of Books* 41, no. 12 (1994), http://www.nybooks.com/articles/2189. Accessed August 25, 2006.
73. Kennan, *Memoirs, 1950–1963,* 222.
74. Kennan, *Decline of the West?* 51, 53.

75. Richard Pipes in ibid., 63.

76. Ibid., 67.

77. George F. Kennan, "A Last Warning: Reply to My Critics," *Encounter* 51, no. 1 (1978): 15.

78. Ibid.

79. Ibid., 16.

80. Irving Kristol, "The Neoconservative Persuasion," *Weekly Standard* 8, no. 47 (2003), http://www.weeklystandard.com/Content/Public/Articles/000/000/003/000.tzmlw.asp. Accessed August 29, 2006.

81. Kennan, *At a Century's Ending,* 78.

82. Quoted in Paul Lettow, *Ronald Reagan and His Quest to Abolish Nuclear Weapons* (New York: Random House, 2005), 6.

83. Quoted in ibid., 50.

84. Quoted in ibid., 86.

85. Quoted in John Lewis Gaddis, *The Cold War: A New History* (New York: Penguin Press, 2005), 227.

86. Quoted in Lettow, *Ronald Reagan and His Quest,* 133.

87. Quoted in Gaddis, *The Cold War,* 231.

88. Kennan, *At a Century's Ending,* 228.

89. Quoted in Peter Reddaway, "The Role of Popular Discontent," *National Interest* 31 (1993): 58.

90. Quoted in Robert Conquest, "Academe and the Soviet Myth," *National Interest* 31 (1993): 96.

91. Bernard Levin, "One Who Got it Right," *National Interest* 31 (1993): 64–65.

92. See George F. Kennan, "Witness to the Fall," *New York Review of Books* 42, no.18 (1995), http://www.nybooks.com/articles/1716. Accessed September 5, 2006.

93. Kennan, *At a Century's Ending,* 296–97.

94. Quoted in Albert Eisele, "Hill Profile: George F. Kennan," *Hill* 25 September 2002, http://www.mtholyoke.edu/acad/intrel/bush/kennan.htm. Accessed September 7, 2006.

95. Quoted in Jane Mayer, "A Doctrine Passes," *New Yorker,* October 14 and 21, 2002, http://www.newyorker.com/printables/talk/021014ta_talk_mayer. Accessed September 7, 2006.

96. Kennan, *Decline of the West?* 36.

97. Kennan, *Around the Cragged Hill,* 36.

98. George F. Kennan, letter to his children on genealogy, April 15, 1961, George F. Kennan Papers, box 20, folder 26.

99. Kennan, *Around the Cragged Hill,* 49.

100. George F. Kennan, sermon for Protestant Church Group Service, Belgrade, Yugoslavia, October 1, 1961, George F. Kennan Papers, box 20, folder 29.

101. George F. Kennan, "The Relation of Religion to Government," *Princeton Seminary Bulletin* 62, no. 1 (1969): 45.
102. Kennan, *Around the Cragged Hill,* 39.
103. Ibid., 40.
104. Quoted in John Wilson, "Dr. Z," http://www.christianitytoday.com/books/features/bccorner/031103.html. Accessed August 29, 2007.
105. Donald Davie, *The Poems of Dr. Zhivago* (Manchester: Manchester University Press, 1965), 149.
106. Kennan, *Around the Cragged Hill,* 49.
107. Ibid.
108. Ibid., 39.

## Three: Traditions of Thought

1. Kennan, *Around the Cragged Hill,* 251.
2. Quoted in Henry Kissinger, *Diplomacy* (New York: Simon and Schuster, 1994), 125, 129.
3. Quoted in Hans J. Morgenthau, *In Defense of the National Interest* (Lanham, MD: University Press of America, 1982 [1951]), 15–16.
4. Quoted in George F. Kennan, "On American Principles," *Foreign Affairs* 74, no. 2 (1995): 118.
5. Morgenthau, *In Defense of the National Interest,* 4.
6. Ibid., 33.
7. Edmund Burke, *Reflections on the Revolution in France,* ed. Conor Cruise O'Brien (New York: Penguin Books, 1968 [1790]), 125.
8. Morgenthau, *In Defense of the National Interest,* 109.
9. Ibid., 116.
10. Quoted in Richard L. Russell, *George F. Kennan's Strategic Thought: The Making of an American Political Realist* (Westport, CT: Praeger, 1999), 10.
11. Quoted in Christoph Frei, *Hans J. Morgenthau: An Intellectual Biography* (Baton Rouge, LA: Louisiana State University Press, 2001), 112.
12. George F. Kennan, sermon for Protestant Church Group Service, Belgrade, Yugoslavia, March 17, 1963, George F. Kennan Papers, box 20, folder 36.
13. Quoted in Richard Wightman Fox, *Reinhold Niebuhr: A Biography* (New York: Pantheon Books, 1985), 215.
14. Reinhold Niebuhr, *The Nature and Destiny of Man: A Christian Interpretation,* I (New York: Charles Scribner's Sons, 1949), 145.
15. Ibid., 17.
16. Reinhold Niebuhr, *The Irony of American History* (New York: Charles Scribner's Sons, 1952), 19, 71.

17. Ibid., 133.
18. Kennan, *Memoirs, 1925–1950,* 415.
19. Kennan, *The Nuclear Delusion,* 42.
20. George F. Kennan, *Realities of American Foreign Policy* (New York: W. W. Norton, 1966 [1954]), 48.
21. Kennan, *American Diplomacy,* 88.
22. Letter, George F. Kennan to the *New York Times,* August 18, 1952, George F. Kennan Papers, box 29, folder 5.
23. Kennan, *Around the Cragged Hill,* 183.
24. Quoted in Kennan, *Russia and the West Under Lenin and Stalin,* 130.
25. Kennan, *Around the Cragged Hill,* 69.
26. Kennan, *Decline of the West?* 27.
27. Kennan, *The Nuclear Delusion,* 63.
28. Burke, *Reflections,* 228.
29. Kennan, *Around the Cragged Hill,* 120–21.
30. Quoted by George F. Kennan, unused draft, George F. Kennan Papers, box 26, folder 1-E-2, Annex IV.
31. Kennan, *Sketches from a Life,* 239.
32. George F. Kennan, "'That Candles May Be Brought. . . .'" *Encounter* 16, no. 2 (1961): 74.
33. *Interviews with George F. Kennan,* ed. T. Christopher Jespersen (Jackson, MS: University Press of Mississippi, 2002), 153–54.
34. George F. Kennan, "Foreign Policy and Christian Conscience," *Atlantic Monthly,* May 1959, http://www.theatlantic.com/politics/foreign/gkchri.htm. Accessed May 18, 2004.
35. Kennan, *Russia and the West Under Lenin and Stalin,* 301.
36. Kennan, *From Prague after Munich,* 9.
37. Quoted in Anders Stephanson, *Kennan and the Art of Foreign Policy* (Cambridge, MA: Harvard University Press, 1989), 24.
38. Quoted in Hugh Kay, *Salazar and Modern Portugal* (London: Eyre and Spottiswoode, 1970), 68–69.
39. Quoted in ibid., 67.
40. Kennan, *Democracy and the Student Left,* 180.
41. Oswald Spengler, *The Decline of the West,* I, trans. Charles Francis Atkinson (New York: Alfred A. Knopf, 1926–28), 353.
42. Ibid., 32.
43. Ibid., 27.
44. Ibid., 254.
45. Quoted in the introduction to Edward Gibbon, *The History of the Decline and Fall of the Roman Empire,* I-II, ed. David Womersley (London: Penguin Classics, 1995), xix.
46. Gibbon, *The History of the Decline and Fall of the Roman Empire,* 31.
47. Ibid.

48. Edward Gibbon, "General Observations on the Fall of the Roman Empire in the West," http://www.ccel.org/g/gibbon/decline/volume1/chap39.htm. Accessed February 12, 2007.

49. Ibid.

50. Gibbon, *The History of the Decline and Fall of the Roman Empire*, 489.

51. Ibid., 515, 518, 577.

52. Ibid., 824.

53. Ibid., 876.

54. Gibbon, "General Observations."

55. Kennan, *Sketches from a Life*, 180.

56. George F. Kennan, *America After Vietnam* (Williamsburg, VA: Colonial Williamsburg, 1968), 6, 8.

57. Quoted in Nicholas Lemann, "The Provocateur," *New Yorker* November 13, 2000, 100.

58. Kennan, *Around the Cragged Hill*, 154.

59. Patrick J. Buchanan, *State of Emergency: The Third World Invasion and Conquest of America* (New York: Thomas Dunne Books, 2006), 6.

60. Kennan, *Decline of the West?* 14–15.

61. Kennan, *Sketches from a Life*, 321.

62. George F. Kennan, "To Prevent a World Wasteland: A Proposal," *Foreign Affairs* April 1970, http://www.foreignaffairs.org/19700401faessay48301/george-f-kennan/to-prevent-a-world. . . . Accessed February 27, 2007.

63. Kennan, *At a Century's Ending*, 281.

64. Rachel L. Carson, *The Sea Around Us* (New York: Oxford University Press, 1951), 15.

65. Wendell Berry, *The Unsettling of America: Culture and Agriculture* (San Francisco: Sierra Club Books, 1986 [1977]), 7.

66. Carson, *The Sea Around Us*, 172.

67. Kennan, "To Prevent a World Wasteland."

68. Kennan, *Realities of American Foreign Policy*, 109.

69. Kennan, *Sketches from a Life*, 7.

70. Ibid., 172–73.

71. Spengler, *The Decline of the West*, I, 41.

72. Kennan, *Around the Cragged Hill*, 251; see also J. R. R. Tolkien, *The Fellowship of the Ring* (New York: Ballantine Books, 1965), 352.

73. Kennan, *Around the Cragged Hill*, 259.

74. Quoted in John Garth, *Tolkien and the Great War: The Threshold of Middle-Earth* (Boston: Houghton Mifflin, 2003), 312.

75. Quoted in Barton Gellman, *Contending with Kennan: Toward a Philosophy of American Power* (New York: Praeger Publishers, 1984), 31.

76. Ronald Steel, "George Kennan at 100," *New York Review of Books*, April 29, 2004, 8.

77. Letter, George F. Kennan to George Kateb, December 15, 1967, George F. Kennan Papers, box 31, folder 13.
78. Quoted in Lemann, "The Provocateur," 98.
79. Burke, *Reflections*, 90–91.
80. Ibid., 228.
81. Quoted in Lemann, "The Provocateur," 98.
82. Quoted in Melvin J. Lasky, "A Conversation with George Kennan," *Encounter* 14, no. 3 (1960): 50.
83. Quoted in Kennan, *Around the Cragged Hill*, 13.
84. John Crowe Ransom in Twelve Southerners, *I'll Take My Stand: The South and the Agrarian Tradition* (New York: Harper and Row, 1962 [1930]), 3.
85. Letter, George F. Kennan to "Frank," March 23, 1964, George F. Kennan Papers, box 31, folder 10.
86. Andrew Nelson Lytle in *I'll Take My Stand*, 205.
87. Kennan, *Around the Cragged Hill*, 102.
88. Kennan, *Memoirs, 1950–1963*, 128.
89. Kennan, *Sketches from a Life*, 163.
90. Robert Penn Warren, *Brother to Dragons: A Tale in Verse and Voices* (New York: Random House, 1953), 190.
91. Letter, George F. Kennan to William F. Buckley, Jr. (not sent), November 4, 1960, George F. Kennan Papers, box 27, folder 1-E-21.
92. John Lukacs, *Confessions of an Original Sinner* (New York: Ticknor and Fields, 1990), 302.

## Conclusion: "Mistress"

1. Kennan, *Memoirs, 1950–1963*, 130.
2. Kennan, *The Fateful Alliance*, xvii.
3. Ibid., xix.
4. Kennan, *Sketches from a Life*, 6–7.
5. George F. Kennan, "History as Literature," *Encounter* 12, no. 4 (1959): 12.
6. Kennan, *Soviet-American Relations, I: Russia Leaves the War*, 3.
7. Ibid., 68–69.
8. Kennan, "History as Literature," 13, 15.
9. Kennan, *Soviet-American Relations, II: The Decision to Intervene*, 469.
10. C. V. Wedgwood, *Edward Gibbon* (London: Longmans, Green, 1955), 10.
11. Kennan, *The Fateful Alliance*, 241.
12. Kennan, *An American Family*, 19.
13. Lukacs, *Confessions*, 40.

14. Kennan, "History as Literature," 16; *At a Century's Ending,* 304.
15. Kennan, "History as Literature," 16.
16. George F. Kennan, "It's History, But is It Literature?" *New York Times Book Review,* April 26, 1959, p. 35.
17. Ibid.
18. Kennan, "History as Literature," 14.
19. George F. Kennan, statement at National Book Awards Ceremony, March 6, 1968, George F. Kennan Papers, box 22, folder 18.
20. José Ortega y Gasset, *The Revolt of the Masses,* trans. Anthony Kerrigan (Notre Dame, IN: University of Notre Dame Press, 1985), 76.
21. George F. Kennan, Presidential Address to the American Academy of Arts and Letters, May 28, 1968, George F. Kennan Papers, box 14, folder 1-B-159.
22. Quoted in Lemann, "The Provocateur," 100.
23. Kennan, *Democracy and the Student Left,* 189.
24. Kennan, *Memoirs, 1925–1950,* 37.
25. Interviews with Liz Stenard and Terri Bramley, Princeton, July 2007.
26. Lukacs, *George Kennan,* 5.

# Bibliography

## Unpublished Sources

Collection

George F. Kennan Papers, Public Policy Papers, Department of Rare Books and Special Collections, Princeton University Library.

Interviews

Terri Bramley, Princeton, July 2007.
Liz Stenard, Princeton, July 2007.

## Published Sources

Books by George F. Kennan

*America After Vietnam.* Williamsburg: Colonial Williamsburg, 1968.
*American Diplomacy, 1900–1950.* New York: Mentor Books, 1951.
*An American Family: The Kennans—The First Three Generations.* New York: W. W. Norton, 2000.
*Around the Cragged Hill: A Personal and Political Philosophy.* New York: W. W. Norton, 1993.
*At a Century's Ending: Reflections, 1982–1995.* New York: W. W. Norton, 1996.
*The Cloud of Danger: Current Realities of American Foreign Policy.* Boston: Little, Brown, 1977.

*The Decline of Bismarck's European Order: Franco-Russian Relations, 1875–1890.* Princeton, NJ: Princeton University Press, 1979.
*Decline of the West? George Kennan and His Critics.* Edited by Martin F. Herz. Washington, DC: Ethics and Public Policy Center, 1978.
*Democracy and the Student Left.* New York: Bantam Books, 1968.
*The Fateful Alliance: France, Russia, and the Coming of the First World War.* New York: Pantheon Books, 1984.
*From Prague after Munich: Diplomatic Papers, 1938–1940.* Princeton, NJ: Princeton University Press, 1968.
*Interviews with George F. Kennan.* Edited by T. Christopher Jespersen. Jackson, MS: University Press of Mississippi, 2002.
*The Marquis de Custine and His Russia in 1839.* Princeton, NJ: Princeton University Press, 1971.
*Measures Short of War: The George F. Kennan Lectures at the National War College, 1946–47.* Edited by Giles D. Harlow and George C. Maerz. Washington, DC: National Defense University Press, 1991.
*Memoirs, 1950–1963.* Boston: Little, Brown, 1972.
*Memoirs, 1925–1950.* Boston: Little, Brown, 1967.
*The Nuclear Delusion: Soviet-American Relations in the Atomic Age.* New York: Pantheon Books, 1983.
*Realities of American Foreign Policy.* New York: W. W. Norton, 1966 [1954].
*Russia, the Atom, and the West: The BBC Reith Lectures, 1957.* London: Oxford University Press, 1958.
*Russia and the West Under Lenin and Stalin.* New York: Mentor, 1961.
*Sketches from a Life.* New York: Pantheon Books, 1989.
*Soviet-American Relations, 1917–1920, I: Russia Leaves the War.* Princeton, NJ: Princeton University Press, 1956.
*Soviet-American Relations, 1917–1920, II: The Decision to Intervene.* Princeton, NJ: Princeton University Press, 1958.
*Soviet Foreign Policy 1917–1941.* Westport, CT: Greenwood Press, 1960.

## Articles and Papers by George F. Kennan

"The American Student and Foreign Affairs." *New England Association Review* 9, 2 (1961): 12–13, 21–23.
"Between Earth and Hell." *New York Review of Books* 21, 4 (1974), http://www.nybooks.com/articles/9569.
"Causes of the Russian Revolution." *Listener* 78, 2014 (1967): 557–60.
"The Challenge of Freedom." *New Leader* 38, 51 (1955): 11–12.
"A Conversation with George Kennan." Conducted by Melvin J. Lasky. *Encounter* 14, 3 (1960): 46–57.
"Credo of a Civil Servant." *Princeton Alumni Weekly* 54, 16 (1954): 10–13.

"A Different Approach to the World: An Interview." *New York Review of Books* 23 (1977): 21–22.

"The Experience of Writing History." *Virginia Quarterly Review* 36, 2 (1960): 205–14.

"Foreign Policy and Christian Conscience." *Atlantic Monthly* May 1959, http://www.theatlantic.com/politics/foreign/gkchri.htm.

"From World War to Cold War." With John Lukacs. *American Heritage* 46, 8 (1995): 42–44, 48, 50, 52, 54, 56, 58–60, 62, 64–67.

"An Historian of Potsdam and His Readers." *American Slavic and East European Review* 20, 2 (1961): 289–94.

"History as Literature." *Encounter* 12, 4 (1959): 10–16.

"In Defense of Oppenheimer." *New York Review of Books* 41, 12 (1994), http://www.nybooks.com/articles/2189.

"Interview for CNN Cold War Series." September 27, 1998. http://www.gwu.edu/~nsarchiv/coldwar/interviews/episode-1/Kennan.

"Introducing Eugene McCarthy." *New York Review of Books* 10, 7 (1968), http://www.nybooks.com/articles/11729.

"It's History, But is It Literature?" *New York Times Book Review,* April 26, 1959, 1, 34–35.

"A Last Warning: Reply to My Critics." *Encounter* 51, 1 (1978): 15–18.

"A Letter on Germany." *New York Review of Books* 45, 19 (1998): 19–21.

"Memorandum for the Minister." *New York Review of Books* 48, 7 (2001): 23.

"Noble Man." *New York Review of Books* 20, 4 (1973), http://www.nybooks.com/articles/9906.

"On American Principles." *Foreign Affairs* 74, 2 (1995): 116–26.

"On Nuclear War." *New York Review of Books* 28, 21–22 (1982), http://www.nybooks.com/articles/6761.

"On 'Speak Truth to Power.'" *Progressive,* October 1955, pp. 16–18.

"Oppenheimer." *Encounter* 28, 4 (1967): 55–56.

"Policy Planning Staff/1: Policy with Respect to American Aid to Western Europe." *Foreign Relations of the United States,* III (1947): 223–30.

"Polycentrism and Western Policy." http://www.foreignaffairs.org/19640101faessay42201-po/george-f-kennan/polycentrism-an. . . .

"PPS Memorandum: Inauguration of Organized Political Warfare." May 4, 1948. http://academic.brooklyn.cuny.edu/history/johnson/65ciafounding3.htm.

"The Relation of Religion to Government." *Princeton Seminary Bulletin* 62, 1 (1969): 42–47.

"Report, the Internment and Repatriation of the American Official Group in Germany—1941–1942." *American Foreign Service Journal,* August 1942, pp. 422–26, 456–59; September 1942, pp. 473–77, 502–507.

"Report on Latin America." *Foreign Relations of the United States,* 1950, II, 598–624.

"Spy and Counterspy." *New York Times,* May 18, 1997.

"'That Candles May Be Brought. . . .'" *Encounter* 16, 2 (1961): 72–74.

"To Be or Not To Be a Christian," *Christianity and Crisis,* May 3, 1954, pp. 51–53.

"To Prevent a World Wasteland: A Proposal." *Foreign Affairs,* April 1970, http://www.foreignaffairs.org/19700401faessay48301/george-f-kennan/ to-prevent-a-world. . . .

"Totalitarianism in the Modern World." In *Totalitarianism.* Ed. Carl J. Friedrich. New York: Grosset and Dunlop, 1964, pp. 17–36.

"The Value of a St. John's Education." *Speeches of Significance Climaxing the 75th Anniversary Commencement.* Delafield, Wisconsin: St. John's Military Academy, 1960, pp. 3–9.

"Why Do I Hope?" *Progressive* 31, 5 (1967): 26–28.

"Witness to the Fall." *New York Review of Books* 42, 18 (1995), http://www. nybooks.com/articles/1716.

## Other Primary Sources

Aron, Raymond. *Memoirs: Fifty Years of Political Reflection.* Translated by George Holoch. New York: Holmes & Meier, 1990.

Berry, Wendell. *The Unsettling of America: Culture and Agriculture.* San Francisco: Sierra Club Books, 1986 [1977].

Bullitt, Orville H., ed. *For the President: Personal and Secret: Correspondence Between Franklin D. Roosevelt and William C. Bullitt.* Boston: Houghton Mifflin, 1972.

Bullitt, William C. "The Size of a Banana," *National Review* 2, 29 (1956): 14–15.

Burke, Edmund. *Reflections on the Revolution in France.* Edited by Conor Cruise O'Brien. New York: Penguin Books, 1968 [1790].

Burnham, James. *Containment or Liberation? An Inquiry into the Aims of United States Foreign Policy.* New York: John Day, 1953.

Carson, Rachel L. *The Sea Around Us.* New York: Oxford University Press, 1951.

Chekhov, Anton. *The Island: A Journey to Sakhalin.* Translated by Luba and Michael Terpak. New York: Washington Square Press, 1967.

———. *The Steppe and Other Stories.* Translated by Ronald Hingley. Oxford: Oxford University Press, 1998.

———. *The Stories.* New York: Modern Library, 1959.

Fitzgerald, F. Scott. *The Great Gatsby.* New York: Scribner Paperback Fiction, 1995 [1925].

———. *This Side of Paradise.* New York: Charles Scribner's Sons, 1920.

Freud, Sigmund. *Civilization and Its Discontents.* Translated and edited by James Strachey. New York: W. W. Norton, 1962.

Gibbon, Edward. "General Observations on the Fall of the Roman Empire in the West." http://www.ccel.org/g/gibbon/decline/volume1/chap39.htm.

————. *The Decline and Fall of the Roman Empire*, vols. I-III. New York: Modern Library, n.d.

————. *The History of the Decline and Fall of the Roman Empire*, I-II. Edited by David Womersley. London: Penguin Books, 1995 [1776–88].

Institute for Advanced Study. *Annual Report for the Fiscal Year July 1, 1981-June 30, 1982*. Princeton, NJ: The Institute for Advanced Study, 1982.

Kennan, George. *Siberia and the Exile System*. Introduced by George Frost Kennan. Chicago: University of Chicago Press, 1958 [1891].

————. *Tent Life in Siberia: An Incredible Account of Adventure, Travel, and Survival*. New York: Skyhorse, 2007 [1870].

Klehr, Harvey, Haynes, John Earl, and Firsov, Fridrikh Igorevich. *The Secret World of American Communism*. New Haven, CT: Yale University Press, 1995.

Kristol, Irving. "The Neoconservative Persuasion." *Weekly Standard* 8, 47 (2003), http://www.weeklystandard.com/Content/Public/Articles/000/000/003/000tzmlw.asp.

Lasky, Melvin J. (ed.). *The West, the Atom, and Russia: A Round-Table Discussion of the Views of George F. Kennan*. Paris: Congress for Cultural Freedom, 1958.

Lippmann, Walter. *The Cold War: A Study in U.S. Foreign Policy*. New York: Harper and Brothers, 1947.

Lukacs, John. *Confessions of an Original Sinner*. New York: Ticknor and Fields, 1990.

Marshall, George C. "The Marshall Plan Speech." http://www.georgecmarshall.org/lt/speeches/marshall_plan.cfm.

Morgenthau, Hans J. *In Defense of the National Interest*. Lanham, MD: University Press of America, 1982 [1951].

————. *Politics Among Nations: The Struggle for Power and Peace*. Second Edition. New York: Alfred A. Knopf, 1958.

Niebuhr, Reinhold. *The Irony of American History*. New York: Charles Scribner's Sons, 1952.

————. *The Nature and Destiny of Man: A Christian Interpretation*. New York: Charles Scribner's Sons, 1949.

Ortega y Gasset, José. *The Revolt of the Masses*. Translated by Anthony Kerrigan. Notre Dame, IN: University of Notre Dame Press, 1985 [1930].

Pasternak, Boris. *Doctor Zhivago*. Translated by Max Hayward and Manya Harari. New York: Pantheon Books, 1958.

Pipes, Richard, ed. *The Unknown Lenin: From the Secret Archive*. With the assistance of David Brandenberger. Translated by Catherine A. Fitzpatrick. New Haven, CT: Yale University Press, 1996.

Spengler, Oswald. *The Decline of the West*, I-II. Translated by Charles Francis Atkinson. New York: Alfred A. Knopf, 1926–28.
Teller, Edward. *Memoirs: A Twentieth-Century Journey in Science and Politics*. With Judith Shoolery. Cambridge, MA: Perseus, 2001.
*The Institute Letter*. Institute for Advanced Study. Winter 2007.
Tolkien, J.R.R. *The Fellowship of the Ring*. New York: Ballantine Books, 1965.
Twelve Southerners. *I'll Take My Stand: The South and the Agrarian Tradition*. New York: Harper and Row, 1962 [1930].
Unamuno, Miguel de. *Tragic Sense of Life*. Translated by J.E. Crawford Flitch. New York: Dover Publications, 1954 [1921].
Warren, Robert Penn. *Brother to Dragons: A Tale in Verse and Voices*. New York: Random House, 1953.
Wedgwood, C. V. *Literature and the Historian*. London: The English Association, 1956.
Wvong, Russil. "George F. Kennan on the Web." http://www.geocities.com/rwvong/future/kennan.html.

## Secondary Sources

Associated Press. "Yugoslavs Ponder Kennan's Role." *Christian Science Monitor*, July 18, 1961.
Bacevich, Andrew J. "Prophets and Poseurs: Niebuhr and Our Times." *World Affairs* 170, 3 (2008): 24–37.
Barzun, Jacques. *From Dawn to Decadence: 500 Years of Western Cultural Life, 1500 to the Present*. New York: HarperCollins, 2000.
Beum, Robert. "The Divinization of Democracy," *Modern Age*. 49, 2 (2007): 120–29.
Bird, Kai, and Sherwin, Martin J. *American Prometheus: The Triumph and Tragedy of J. Robert Oppenheimer*. New York: Alfred A. Knopf, 2005.
Buchanan, Patrick J. *State of Emergency: The Third World Invasion and Conquest of America*. New York: Thomas Dunne Books, 2006.
————. *The Death of the West: How Dying Populations and Immigrant Invasions Imperil Our Country and Civilization*. New York: Thomas Dunne, 2002.
Burdick, Charles B. *An American Island in Hitler's Reich: The Bad Nauheim Internment*. Menlo Park, CA: Markgraf Publications Group, 1987.
Burrow, J. W. *Gibbon*. Oxford: Oxford University Press, 1985.
Coleman, Peter. *The Liberal Conspiracy: The Congress for Cultural Freedom and the Struggle for the Mind of Postwar Europe*. New York: The Free Press, 1989.
Congdon, Lee. "Kuehnelt-Leddihn, Erik von (1909–99)." *American Conservatism: An Encyclopedia*. Edited by Bruce Frohnen, Jeremy Beer, and Jeffrey O. Nelson. Wilmington, Delaware: ISI Books, 2006, pp. 483–84.

————. *Seeing Red: Hungarian Intellectuals in Exile and the Challenge of Communism.* DeKalb, IL: Northern Illinois University Press, 2001.

————. "The Realist Kennan." *American Conservative* 5, 22 (2006): 21–23.

Conquest, Robert. "Academe and the Soviet Myth." *National Interest* 31 (1993): 91–98.

————. *The Great Terror: A Reassessment.* New York: Oxford University Press, 1990.

Davie, Donald. *The Poems of Dr. Zhivago.* Manchester: Manchester University Press, 1965.

Eisele, Albert. "Hill Profile: George F. Kennan." *Hill,* September 25, 2002, http://www.mtholyoke.edu/acad/intrel/bush/kennan.htm.

Epstein, Joseph. *Alexis de Tocqueville: Democracy's Guide.* New York: HarperCollins, 2006.

————. *Envy.* New York: New York Public Library and Oxford University Press, 2003.

————. *Partial Payments: Essays on Writers and Their Lives.* New York: W. W. Norton, 1989.

————. "The Author as Character." *Weekly Standard* 9, 45 (2004): 31–35.

Fest, Joachim. *Plotting Hitler's Death: The Story of the German Resistance.* Translated by Bruce Little. New York: Henry Holt, 1996.

Fox, Richard Wightman. *Reinhold Niebuhr: A Biography.* New York: Pantheon Books, 1985.

Frei, Christoph. *Hans J. Morgenthau: An Intellectual Biography.* Baton Rouge, LA: Louisiana State University Press, 2001.

Gaddis, John Lewis. *The Cold War: A New History.* New York: The Penguin Press, 2005.

Garth, John. *Tolkien and the Great War: The Threshold of Middle-Earth.* Boston: Houghton Mifflin, 2003.

Gellman, Barton. *Contending with Kennan: Toward a Philosophy of American Power.* New York: Praeger Publishers, 1984.

Gottfried, Paul. "Morgenthau and Strauss: An Instructive Polarity." In *One Hundred Year Commemoration to the Life of Hans Morgenthau (1904–2004).* Edited by G. O. Mazur. New York: Semenenko Foundation, 2004, pp. 115–31.

Grayling, A. C. *Among the Dead Cities: The History and Moral Legacy of the WW II Bombing of Civilians in Germany and Japan.* New York: Walker and Company, 2006.

Hallman, David A. "The Southern Voice in the Conservative Complaint of Modernist Literature." In *Essays and Reviews.* Harrisonburg: James Madison University, 1992, 65–81.

Hassell, Agostino von, and MacRae, Sigrid (with Simone Ameskamp). *Alliance of Enemies: The Untold Story of the Secret American and German Collaboration to End World War II.* New York: St. Martin's Press, 2006.

Herman, Arthur. *The Idea of Decline in Western History.* New York: Free Press, 1997.

Hingley, Ronald. *Chekhov: A Biographical and Critical Study.* London: George Allen and Unwin, 1950.

Hixson, Walter L. *George F. Kennan: Cold War Iconoclast.* New York: Columbia University Press, 1989.

Howard, Michael. *Clausewitz.* Oxford University Press, 1983.

Isaacson, Walter, and Thomas, Evan. *The Wise Men: Six Friends and the World They Made.* New York: Touchstone, 1988.

Johnson, Paul. *Modern Times: The World from the Twenties to the Nineties.* New York: HarperPerennial, 1991.

Joll, James. "The Old Diplomacy." *New York Review of Books* 26, 21-22 (1980), http://www.nybooks.com/articles/7554.

―――. "Turning Toward War." *New York Review of Books* 31, 18 (1984), http://www.nybooks.com/articles/5660.

Kay, Hugh. *Salazar and Modern Portugal.* London: Eyre and Spottiswoode, 1970.

Kegley, Charles W., and Bretall, Robert W., eds. *Reinhold Niebuhr: His Religious, Social, and Political Thought.* New York: Macmillan Company, 1956.

Kenez, Peter. *Hungary from the Nazis to the Soviets: The Establishment of the Communist Regime in Hungary, 1944-1948.* Cambridge: Cambridge University Press, 2006.

Kissinger, Henry. *Diplomacy.* New York: Simon and Schuster, 1994.

Klemperer, Klemens von. *German Resistance Against Hitler: The Search for Allies Abroad, 1938-1945.* Oxford: Clarendon Press, 1992.

Kuklick, Bruce. *Blind Oracles: Intellectuals and War from Kennan to Kissinger.* Princeton, NJ: Princeton University Press, 2006.

Langer, William L. *European Alliances and Alignments, 1871-1890.* New York: Vintage Books, 1950.

―――. *The Franco-Russian Alliance, 1890-1894.* New York: Octagon Books, 1977 [1929].

Lemann, Nicholas. "The Provocateur." *New Yorker,* November 13, 2000, 94, 96-98, 100.

Lerner, Robert. "Conversations with George Kennan." *Historically Speaking* 6, 6 (2005): 11-13.

Lettow, Paul. *Ronald Reagan and His Quest to Abolish Nuclear Weapons.* New York: Random House, 2005.

Levin, Bernard. "One Who Got it Right." *National Interest* 31 (1993): 64-65.

Lincoln, W. Bruce. *Between Heaven and Hell: The Story of a Thousand Years of Artistic Life in Russia.* New York: Viking, 1998.

―――. *Red Victory: A History of the Russian Civil War.* New York: Simon and Schuster, 1989.

————. *The Conquest of a Continent: Siberia and the Russians.* New York: Random House, 1994.

Lukacs, John. *George Kennan: A Study of Character.* New Haven, CT: Yale University Press, 2007.

————. "George Kennan, Hungary and Changes in Eastern Europe." http://www.hungarianquarterly.com/no184/14.html.

————. *Philadelphia: Patricians and Philistines, 1900–1950.* New York: Farrar, Straus, Giroux, 1981.

McConnell, Scott. "The Good Strategist." *American Conservative* 4, 11 (2005): 7–10.

McDougall, Walter A. *Promised Land, Crusader State: The American Encounter with the World Since 1776.* Boston: Houghton Mifflin, 1997.

McMillan, Priscilla J. *The Ruin of J. Robert Oppenheimer and the Birth of the Modern Arms Race.* New York: Viking, 2005.

Mastny, Vojtech. *The Czechs Under Nazi Rule: The Failure of National Resistance, 1939–1942.* New York: Columbia University Press, 1971.

Mayer, Jane. "A Doctrine Passes." *New Yorker,* October 14 and 21, 2002, http://www.newyorker.com/printables/talk/021014ta_talk_mayer.

Mayers, David. *George Kennan and the Dilemmas of US Foreign Policy.* New York: Oxford University Press, 1988.

Miscamble, Wilson D. *George F. Kennan and the Making of American Foreign Policy, 1947–1950.* Princeton, NJ: Princeton University Press, 1992.

Nicolson, Harold. *The Evolution of Diplomacy.* New York: Collier Books, 1962.

Nisbet, Robert. *The Present Age: Progress and Anarchy in Modern America.* New York: Harper and Row, 1989.

Oberdorfer, Don. *Princeton University: The First 250 Years.* Princeton, NJ: Princeton University, 1995.

Pelikan, Jaroslav. *The Excellent Empire: The Fall of Rome and the Triumph of the Church.* San Francisco: Harper and Row, 1987.

Reddaway, Peter. "The Role of Popular Discontent." *National Interest* 31 (1993): 57–63.

Rossiter, Clinton. *Conservatism in America: The Thankless Persuasion.* Second Edition. New York: Alfred A. Knopf, 1962.

Russell, Richard L. *George F. Kennan's Strategic Thought: The Making of an American Political Realist.* Westport, CT: Praeger, 1999.

Schecter, Jerrold and Leona. *Sacred Secrets: How Soviet Intelligence Operations Changed American History.* Washington, DC: Brassey's, 2002.

Smith, Michael Joseph. *Realist Thought from Weber to Kissinger.* Baton Rouge, LA: Louisiana State University Press, 1986.

Steel, Ronald. "George Kennan at 100." *New York Review of Books* 51, 7 (2004): 8–9.

————. "Man Without a Country," *New York Review of Books,* 9, 12 (1968): 8–13.

Stephanson, Anders. *Kennan and the Art of Foreign Policy.* Cambridge, MA: Harvard University Press, 1989.

Stromberg, Roland N. *Democracy: A Short, Analytical History.* Armonk, NY: M. E. Sharpe, 1996.

Thompson, Kenneth W. *Political Realism and the Crisis of World Politics: An American Approach to Foreign Policy.* Washington, DC: University Press of America, 1982 [1960].

Treadgold, Donald W. "George Kennan's Neo-Isolationism," *New Leader,* September 3, 1956, 9–11.

Volkogonov, Dmitri. *Lenin: A New Biography.* Translated and edited by Harold Shukman. New York: Free Press, 1994.

———. *Stalin: Triumph and Tragedy.* Translated and edited by Harold Shukman. New York: Grove Weidenfeld, 1991.

Wedgwood, C. V. *Edward Gibbon.* London: Longmans, Green, 1955.

Wilson, John. "Dr. Z." http://www.christianitytoday.com/books/features/bccorner/031103.html.

Wood, Gordon S. "All in the Family." *New York Review of Books* 48, 3 (2001): 11–12.

# Index